Ann Ivinney-
1984.

.... SOME SUNNY DAY ....
Eileen Whiteing

Woodcote Road, Wallington, looking north, in the late 1930s.

...SOME SUNNY DAY...

Reminiscences of a young wife
in the Second World War

EILEEN WHITEING

London Borough of Sutton Libraries and Arts Services

First published 1983
© 1983 London Borough of Sutton Libraries and Arts Services
Central Library, St. Nicholas Way, Sutton. Surrey, SM1 1EA.
Tel: 01-661 5050

ISBN 0 907335 07 1

Design: Shirley Edwards

Printed by
Alam Printing Services, 147 Gander Green Lane, Sutton, Surrey.
Tel: 01-644 0623/4

CONTENTS

ILLUSTRATIONS ACKNOWLEDGEMENTS

Sources of photographs and other illustrations used are as follows, and thanks are given to those concerned.

Front cover photograph; pages 9, 12, 16, 17, 21, 28, 33, 36, 40, 42, 64, 70, 81: the author.

Frontispiece (ii); pages viii, 3, 6, 8, 23, 25, 27, 30, 58, 69, 73, 74: Local Collection, London Borough of Sutton Libraries and Arts Services.

Pages 5, 15: Croydon Public Libraries

Pages 36, 39: Lancashire Libraries

Page 47: City of Manchester Cultural Services

Map pages 83 & 84: Reproduced by permission of Geographers' A-Z Map Company Ltd. Based on the O.S. map with the sanction of the Controller of H.M. Stationery Office. Crown Copyright Reserved.

Back cover: A design by Fougasse for the front cover of a war-time recipe book.

AUTHOR'S NOTE

We'll meet again
Don't know where,
Don't know when,
But I know we'll meet again
Some sunny day.
Keep smiling through
Just like you used to do
Till the blue skies
Drive the grey clouds far away.

Forty years on, the sound of Dame Vera Lynn singing her famous song instantly revives personal memories of the Second World War, and this book is one ordinary woman's account of those years and how they affected her life. At that time every chain-store was churning out this particular record non-stop, and the poignant words and music somehow seemed very comforting to those who were about to part from loved ones, 'for the duration' or longer, or for ever. I dedicate my story to the memory of all who did not grow old, as we who were left have grown old.

My thanks are specially due to my husband for helping to refresh my memory from time to time with extra details, and to my friends who encouraged me to undertake the book.

January, 1983.

WHITE POSTS, BEDDINGTON.

White Posts, Beddington, where the author first met her future husband at a debating society meeting.

PART I: PRELUDE TO WAR

CHAPTER ONE: 1938

Reading through my diary for the year nineteen thirty-eight, I realise that this promised to be one of the happiest of my life so far, since I had recently become engaged to Dennis and was still thrilled at the sight of the diamond ring proudly displayed on the third finger of my left hand.

We had first met a year or so previously at a meeting of a local debating society held in a small hall known as White Posts, situated on the corner of Guy Road and Croydon Road, Wallington. I think that Dennis had been encouraged to join our membership through the persuasions of a mutual friend, the late Geoffrey Ryder of Osmond Gardens, who subsequently became Deputy Clerk to the Carshalton Urban District Council. Dennis and I soon found we had many interests in common; and, as time went by, our friendship blossomed into romance, as they say. One special event I well recall was when we attended the annual dinner-dance organised by the Wallington Branch of NALGO (then standing for the National Association of Local Government Officers). This was held in the restaurant known as Zeta's, in George Street, Croydon, and was an occasion for full evening dress for both sexes. After a lavish menu of several courses, followed by various speeches and toasts, we danced to the music of Alan Miller and his band, who could always be relied upon to provide a pleasing selection of waltzes, foxtrots and quick-steps; plus the occasional tango for the more talented among us and several special dances with prizes. Only recently, going through some trunks in the attic, I came across the very evening dress I wore that night, which I must have kept for sentimental reasons all these years. It was of soft mauve crêpe, made in real thirties style, and I remember Dennis brought me a spray of fresh violets and anemones to pin on the bodice just below my left shoulder.

Recalling the dances we went to during this period: these were usually organised by our various tennis clubs; the local Red Cross branch; the Conservatives, and so on, and were held at the small

Wentworth Hall in Ruskin Road, Carshalton, or the new Highfield Hall in Carshalton Road. Later on, after the larger Public Hall was built in Stafford Road, Wallington, most of the main functions were held there. 'Flannel Dances' were popular during the summer months, when everyone was expected to turn up in white or grey flannels, or summer dresses, according to sex. Tickets were always on sale in advance, to discourage gatecrashers on the night; and the refreshments were invariably assorted sandwiches, sausage rolls, cakes, and ices; with lemonade or coffee. Occasionally, there was a licensed bar.

One of the highlights each year in the social calendar was the week that the local Operatic Society performed their very talented shows in the Public Hall. On the last night many local notables would be seen in the front rows, sporting evening dress in honour of the occasion, and mingling with the cast in after-the-show parties back-stage. How we enjoyed the delightful music of such legendary plays as those by Ivor Novello, Noel Coward, or Gilbert and Sullivan. *The Desert Song* and *Bitter-sweet* were ever-popular favourites, and we were very fortunate in having the splendid voices of Emily Gardener, Lallie Hawkins, Sylvia Bryant, and, later, Daphne Kelf. The Society was for many years in the capable hands of Mrs. Lister Guest and her husband, and son Langford, who ran the Conservatoire of Music in Ross Parade and brought much local talent to flower. They lived in a pleasant large house in Woodstock Road.

During the day I was working quite hard at my secretarial and editorial job with a small local publishing firm, earning about three to four pounds a week — a comparatively good salary in those days; and, as I lived at home with my family, I had plenty to spare for clothes and personal expenses. Dennis was also working locally, at the Town Hall in Wallington, Surrey, where we both lived, which meant that he was soon home in the evenings and we would spend most of our spare time together. Quite often we would just go for a walk or for a cycle ride if the weather was suitable, but at least twice a week it seems we went off to the local cinema (the programmes always changed mid-week) or by bus or trolley-bus to the nearby towns of Croydon or Sutton to visit the larger cinemas or theatres there. Public transport was so reliable

The Odeon Cinema, Wallington, opened in 1934 at the junction of Ross Road and Woodcote Road.

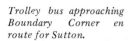

Trolley bus approaching Boundary Corner en route for Sutton.

Plaza Cinema (later the Granada), Carshalton Road, Sutton, showing exterior and interior views.

and so frequent (never more than five or ten minutes to wait between buses) that we thought nothing of visiting friends quite far apart in the same evening, or having supper out, and catching a bus or train home about 10.30 p.m. More importantly, we never had to fear being 'mugged' or raped, as such things were unknown in the areas where we lived, even on dark winter nights.

Enlarging for a moment on the scope of entertainment available to us when we were young, we were certainly lucky to have so many cinemas and theatres available, at reasonable prices and not far away. I recently read in our local newspaper a bitter letter from a teenager who deplored the lack of such amenities, which he said would help to reduce the widespread vandalism and mugging in the streets, often induced by boredom. In Wallington we had the Odeon Cinema, newly-built during the mid-thirties, while further afield we could choose from the many in Sutton and Croydon. The Davis Cinema in North End, Croydon, was palatial in size and luxurious in décor, complete with its famous organ, which ascended for the interlude of about fifteen minutes, then slowly sank into the dimming darkness again, when the programme resumed and the ice-cream girls vanished up the aisles to their appointed places near the back. In Sutton there was the well-known Surrey County Cinema in the High Street and the Plaza (later the Granada), together with what we always called 'the Cheam Road Picture-House'. Most nights in the week, especially Saturdays, there would be long queues of people, patiently waiting in all weathers for their turn to get to the box-office, and firmly controlled by uniformed commissionaires. What joy it was to get into the warm darkness after a wet or cold wait outside, and drift off into a world of escapism!

First time round, of course, my diary records that during 1938 we saw, for instance, Anna Neagle in *Victoria the Great*; Paul Muni and Louise Rainer in *The Good Earth*; *Knight without Armour*; Jean Arthur in *Easy Living*; *A Star is Born*; Jessie Matthews in *Gangway*; *Stage Door*; *Marie Waleska*; Anton Walbrook in *The Rat*; Robert Taylor in *A Yank at Oxford* — and many others, some of which we saw at the Regal Cinema in Purley.

The Croydon Empire often offered a good type of variety show, and it was there that we saw the famous Phyllis Dixey in her

4

The Davis Theatre, High Street, Croydon, decorated for the Coronation of George VI.

original revue; but the great event at that time was to visit the newly-built Streatham Hill Theatre, where we were able to see West End stars in such productions as *Crest of the Wave*, *Balalaika*, *Madame Butterfly* and so on. Buses, as I have said, were plentiful and reliable, so transport was no problem.

For this reason it was quite usual then to do a large part of one's shopping after work in the evening; and a visit to the hairdresser, or the dentist or doctor, had always to be arranged for 'after hours' as it was not normal to be given time off during the day for such things. Many of the small dress shops in Croydon or Sutton were owned by Jewish families who were very hardworking and stayed open most of the evenings, so it was quite easy

5

Woodcote Road, Wallington, looking south. On the right are several shops mentioned by the author. Boots the chemists; Riddington's restaurant (see page 11); and Noble's, the independent chemist, rather hidden, but opposite the second car parked on the right.

to go and buy a new coat or dress then. Sometimes, on my way home from the office, I would wander into Boots, or the independent chemist shop, and spend a pleasant half-hour choosing some new scent or make-up item. Those were the days of the famous Coty fragrances which became very popular, together with 'Ashes of Roses', 'Evening in Paris', 'Tosca', and similar exotic creations.

We were hoping to be married in the summer of 1939, and to this end we both saved as hard as we could towards the cost of our home; and, in my case, my trousseau — a very important item then in any bride-to-be's wedding plans. During our evening walks we therefore greatly enjoyed gazing at the shop windows, particularly the furniture and fashion displays; making endless budgets and plans, trying to decide on colour schemes and so on. Most weeks, too, I managed to buy some small household item to add to my 'bottom drawer', taking great pleasure in crossing off the lists gradually. We also began to keep our eyes open for a likely flat in which to start our married life, since it was quite easy to rent unfurnished accommodation at that time and we were not yet in a position to think about buying a house of our own. In any case, it was our hope that Dennis would, fairly soon, be able to change his job; and we would thus be able to move away into a country or seaside district, in preference to staying all our lives in the London suburbs.

July proved to be very hot and sunny during the second part of the month, and we spent a very happy holiday at Eastbourne, in a pleasant hotel near the sea-front. Swimming and sun-bathing helped most of our days pass lazily by; followed by listening to the band or going to a concert or theatre in the evenings.

But, as summer drifted into autumn, the first dark shadows of trouble on the international scene began to haunt our minds, and dim our happiness, with constant sensational headlines about Hitler and Mussolini, the Fascist dictators of Europe. On September the 8th my diary records: 'Czech crisis very black'; and, on the 14th, I wrote that we were 'very miserable in view of war prospects'. On September the 15th, Mr. Neville Chamberlain, the British Prime Minister, flew to Munich to see Hitler, and for a while things seemed quieter again; but on September 26th the

A photograph of Manor Road, Wallington, looking north, taken from the railway bridge during the 1950s. On the left can be seen the grassed-over tops of the underground public air raid shelters.

Czech crisis was 'worse than ever', to quote my diary, and, on the following Wednesday, we both asked for a morning off in order to see about a Special Marriage Licence, since it was doubtful if peace would be maintained for much longer. By this time, trenches were being dug in parks and playing fields, and gas-masks were being issued to every citizen. On September 29th, however, a last-minute Conference of all the Powers was held in Munich, and my diary records on the following day: 'Peace settled in Europe after all! Much excitement everywhere.' So the special new hat and white kid gloves which I had bought in readiness for an emergency wedding were put away in my bedroom, and life settled down again into its former pleasant routine of work; outings to friends and cinemas; dances; and Christmas celebrations, as autumn wore into winter and that memorable year drew to its close. We were, of course, living in a fool's paradise; but luckily we did not realise it yet and went on making our little plans and pleasures, in blissful ignorance of what was to come in 1939.

8

Ironically, however, on November 11th we both went up to London to watch the Armistice Service at the Cenotaph, from the offices of the Ministry of Health in Whitehall opposite (where Dennis's father was a Senior Civil Servant) and, on our return, the evening papers were announcing that Hitler had invaded the Sudentenland — the shape of things to come, indeed.

Armistice Day service in Whitehall, November 1938 from a window of the Ministry of Health building.

CHAPTER TWO: 1939

January proved to be the normal English mixture of rain, frost and snow, resulting in the usual crop of coughs and colds, with the added gloom, during the last week, of a fresh outbreak of war scares. Nevertheless, we pressed on with our plans for a spring wedding, which, of course, involved inspecting and negotiating a suitable place for us to set up house. Eventually we were lucky in being able to rent a very pleasant maisonette in Melbourne Road, Wallington, and the landlord agreed to have it entirely redecorated to our own choice; much to my delight. Also, it boasted a tiny front and back garden, and I was full of plans for these.

By this time, we were in the throes of choosing carpets and curtains, furniture, and all the necessary household equipment; and I was also going to the dressmaker for fittings of my wedding dress and honeymoon outfit. One weekend, I arrived home from my shopping expedition with a tiny hat composed of (artificial!) Parma violets, shrouded in a fine mauve veil, which was to form part of my going-away ensemble. Incidentally, I still have it, all these years later, as a souvenir of the kind of things we used to wear.

The three-tier wedding cake was ordered, and the menu arranged for the reception following the wedding. Jenny, the family maid, was sent round for one whole day to our new home for the express purpose of cleaning up all the floors after the decorators had left — which just proves how helpless I must have been as regards housework in those days! Towards the middle of March, my diary records further crises of impending war; but we pushed them to the back of our minds and kept hoping for the best, though at least half expecting the worst. In fact, on Good Friday, April 7th (the day before our wedding), we were greeted with the news that Albania had been invaded by Italy, and things looked very black indeed (to quote my diary).

However, April the 8th dawned a day full of blue skies and warm sunshine, and I can still recall the scent of my bouquet of all-white flowers, which arrived early that morning from the same florists who had made up my Mother's wedding flowers nearly thirty years earlier.

Our wedding service was fully choral, complete with the bells being rung; and I remember my surprise at seeing the church so full of our relatives and friends, which was doubtless because my parents and grandparents had lived in the district for a great many years. My four bridesmaids (two sisters and two school-friends) looked delightful in long dresses of pale green organdie – a popular material at that time – and our respective parents added further touches of colour and formality in their splendid outfits in honour of the occasion. After the reception which followed the service, we changed into our 'going-away clothes' and were driven to Croydon to catch the late afternoon train to Eastbourne, which was a favourite place for honeymoons in those days. Confetti was scattered everywhere, and we finally got ourselves installed in the chosen compartment amid the laughter, and cries of good luck, from the special friends who waved us off.

And what a glorious week of early summer weather blessed us on that honeymoon, so that we were able to sunbathe on the beach, and enjoy to the full the sea and countryside of the Sussex coast; with plenty of theatres and concerts in the evenings, and the luxury of staying in a really good hotel which specialised in excellent meals. But, all too soon, our week was over (we intended to have a further week's holiday later in the summer) and we returned to take up our married life in earnest.

Once installed in our own home, I returned to my work as secretary and editorial assistant, and joined my husband for lunch each day at our local restaurant, Riddingtons. It is typical of those times that I felt it necessary to employ a daily help to come in and do the housework for me, so that our evenings were free for leisure and entertaining! I used to do most of my household shopping on Saturday mornings, and was soon in my element making my first cake and entertaining various members of our families and friends to evening meals, so that they might inspect the flat and view all our wedding presents.

And so the summer months passed by, with the usual mixture of heatwaves alternating with cold and showery spells. Quite

11

Wedding day picture, taken outside Holy Trinity Church, Wallington, April 8th 1939.

12

often, at the week-ends, we would drive down to the coast, or out to the countryside, with my parents or in-laws, and, during June, we attended the weddings of my sister Joan, and my cousin Betty, with occasional visits to local fêtes added to our social activities. By August 21st, however, my diary records that the crisis in Europe was starting up again; and by the 24th the news from Danzig was 'very bad' and we were all preparing for the worst. During the following week-end and subsequent week the crisis remained very black, though negotiations were attempted to solve it. We continued our normal daily lives; but in certain areas evacuation began on the 1st of September – and on that very day Germany invaded Poland. My diary reads: 'So that's that. Tea with Dennis's family and stayed the night owing to the immediate black-out'. The next day we returned to our flat in order to pack up some clothes and then went back to my in-laws as it was felt we might be safer there than in our upstairs flat. That entire evening was spent making curtains to black out every window: we had been out early in the morning buying any kind of black or dark brown material, or cardboard, etc., that was available; as it had already become almost unobtainable overnight, owing to the huge demand.

The fateful Sunday, September 3rd, proved to be a glorious day as regards weather; but during the morning war was officially declared with Germany, and we experienced two false alarms of air raids very soon after that, naturally giving us all some nasty frights, though we continued to sit in the garden, and went for a walk in the evening sunshine.

The next day, Monday, saw us both back to work as usual, as our planned holiday in Bournemouth was, of course, cancelled. The weather for the whole week following proved to be glorious summer, and all seemed quiet, so we went for walks or cycle rides in the evenings until darkness fell and imposed the black-out in streets and houses. The following Sunday we both went on duty at the Town Hall Report Centre from two o'clock until ten p.m. – 'very tiring' according to my diary! The duties mainly consisted of sitting about waiting for something to happen; but as this was the 'Phoney War' period, nothing did.

A domestic crisis soon developed, however, when it was learned

13

that my in-laws' house in Foresters Drive, where we were staying, was to be requisitioned by the R.A.F. in order to accommodate men from the Croydon Airport which adjoined the back garden. My in-laws were greatly distressed at the prospect, but there was no appeal, and they had to start house-hunting immediately, to find suitable premises which could be rented. It was therefore decided that the best thing was for us to return to our own flat, which we did at the end of the week, and spent most of the week-end blacking out windows, and so on.

On September 18th Russia also invaded Poland, but I note that we continued our normal lives, and, in fact, went twice to the cinema that week! My diary records that on the 28th Russia signed a military pact with Germany; but, as summer drifted into autumn, and autumn merged into winter, life appears to have been more or less normal, with twice-weekly visits to the cinema, visits to friends, and occasional weddings to attend. On December the 2nd, Dennis began to dig up a space in our small back garden in order to accommodate our Anderson air-raid shelter — a job he completed about three weeks later, and for which we were more than thankful later on, when the air raids began. Christmas seems to have followed the usual pattern of family gatherings and present-giving, even including a visit to *Dick Whittington* at Croydon on Boxing Day. And, as a fitting accompaniment to this momentous year, ice and snow swiftly followed the festivities, until the calendar showed 1940, and we wondered what the future was going to hold for us.

High Street, Croydon: (above) looking south; (below) looking north; showing the Grand Theatre, where Dick Whittington was performed on Boxing Day 1939.

PART II: THE CONFLICT

CHAPTER THREE: 1940

The New Year opened with ice and fog, plus a sore throat for me, which was slow to disappear on account of the usual January weather of frosts and snowfalls. About the middle of the month Dennis completed the floor (planks of wood on a frame) in our Anderson shelter in the back garden. Meanwhile, the weather got steadily worse, resulting in a good deal of illness and frozen pipes, and my diary for the 29th of January records 'the worst snow hold-up in memory'. Nevertheless, we still managed to get to the cinema several times that month, and by the first week of February there was a hint of spring in the air, as I wrote that 'three snowdrops are in bloom'. I was still going daily to my office; and enjoying as well my new domestic duties, such as marmalade-making while sugar supplies were still plentiful.

The Anderson air-raid shelter in the garden of 54 Melbourne Road, Wallington, the house which was the author's first home after her marriage.

The home of Mr. and Mrs. Whiteing senior, in Foresters Drive, Wallington. The house was damaged when a Blenheim bomber crashed on the house next door in February 1940.

Saturday, February 24th, began as a lovely day, and we went into Sutton in the afternoon for shopping and afternoon tea at the Plaza Cinema, together with Dennis's parents. We all returned to the Foresters Drive house to spend the evening and have supper, little dreaming of the tragic event that was to take place there at 6.45 p.m., when an R.A.F. Blenheim bomber took off on a night-training flight from Croydon Aerodrome (which adjoined the back garden), failed to gain height, and crashed on to the house next door. The wing of the plane demolished the corner of our own house, the actual wing-tip finishing up on the spare-room bed. The engine from this wing landed in the front garden next door, setting fire to that house and seriously injuring the wife and small daughter, both of whom died a few days later from severe burns. The rest of the plane finished up on the garages opposite. The pilot, who was alone, was thrown clear but did not survive his injuries. As can be imagined, the noise of the explosion startled us all, and set the dog barking; so my husband and father-in-law rushed to the front door to see what had happened, and then ran

17

into the back garden to render what help they could to the occupants of the burning house.

My father-in-law managed to scramble over the fence into the back garden and assisted the shocked neighbours from the back of their burning house. Mrs. Bridge's clothes had been badly burnt and she had to be swathed in my husband's winter overcoat. Subsequently, she and her husband and the two children were taken to hospital. Meanwhile, my husband fixed up the garden hose and began spraying our garage, as burning embers were by then falling on it; and, by so doing, luckily managed to avoid the fire spreading to our own house. The R.A.F. Fire Service from the airfield arrived quickly on the scene when it was realised what a disaster had occurred, together with the local fire brigade and the auxiliary service.

It is not hard to imagine that, after such a tragic and devastating experience as this, we all felt very shattered during the days that followed; and, in fact, we were both given the Monday off from our offices in order to recover somewhat. It was, of course, a fore-taste of what air raids achieved, in loss of life, and damage to property, as the months went by and the real Battle of Britain took place.

Meanwhile, our daily life went on as usual, and my husband's parents stayed with various friends in the district while their house was being repaired from the crash damage. Eventually, however, the requisitioning of the property by the R.A.F., for use as billets for airmen from the airfield adjoining took place, so they were obliged to find another house to rent temporarily, and they finally settled down again in Ashcombe Road overlooking Carshalton Park.

Easter came early that year, and, in an effort to cheer ourselves up, we decided, together with my parents and two friends, to book-up to spend the holiday week-end in Eastbourne. It was showery when we left on the Thursday by train from East Croydon, but it turned sunny and fine during the week-end, so that we were able to enjoy walking up to Beachy Head, or sitting on the front listening to the band — it was obviously a case of 'business as usual' so far, in this war! We went to a concert on

Sunday evening, having been to church at St. Saviour's in the morning, and eventually returned home during the Monday evening in a packed-out train.

Spring slowly drifted into early summer, and normal life was punctuated by grave news about the invasion of Denmark and Norway by Germany in April, to be followed by the invasion of Holland and Belgium in early May. The weather was hot and sunny, but the news overshadowed everything, and, in fact, a day of National Prayer was organised for Sunday, May 26th. Two days later, my diary records 'Awful sensation — King Leopold surrendered'. All plans for summer holidays were cancelled officially. At this stage I should, perhaps, point out that, as Dennis was a Local Government Officer, he was in a Reserved Occupation until such time as his age group should be called up for war service; so we just tried to carry on with our daily life as normally as possible meanwhile. I note that, in the middle of June, I had my hair cut and set in the (new at that time) page-boy style, and also bought a very attractive navy blue straw hat in the French Breton style! Ironically, on June 17th, I record that France was now asking for an armistice. Italy had by now also declared war on us; and, although at the time we were hardly aware of what was happening, because of press censorship, the legendary Dunkirk evacuation of our forces had been taking place from May 29th onwards. This period seems to mark the end of the 'phoney' war and the beginning of the real conflict in Britain, for my diary records that on June 24th there was an air raid warning for three hours in the night and we all felt terribly tired the next day, after sleeping in the shelters.

Nevertheless we still went out for short cycle rides in the summer evenings, and paid visits to friends or the cinema, despite the blackout and general anxiety. In early July, for a birthday treat, we went up to London for a meal out and a theatre visit. During 1940, we experienced the first signs of rationing, when such items as meat, bacon, ham were drastically rationed (i.e. one shilling's worth of meat per person per week, plus an occasional tin of corned beef); tea was down to two ounces; no cheese at all; butter and margarine four ounces; sugar twelve ounces, then down to eight; and so on!

During the years to follow there were many ups and downs in the food rationing, too many to describe in detail; but the introduction of the Points System for such things as biscuits, tinned goods, dried fruits, rice and so on was a great help. Cakes and bread were unrationed, as was fish when obtainable; also sausages and offal if one was lucky! Vegetables were fairly plentiful, but such things as bananas and oranges became like gold dust and only available for young children. All forms of sweets and chocolate were also rationed. Jams, marmalade and syrup were limited to only a few ounces per person per month; but dried eggs were quite a help for making puddings or cakes, though milk was very scarce and fresh eggs were limited to about one per person per month!

Looking back from this distance it is almost impossible now to remember just how we did manage to produce any meals at all, as nearly every single item was so reduced in quantity as to be useless. People who worked in factories or offices could have the benefit of unrationed meals in canteens; or if one could afford to eat in a restaurant this was a great help. Schools also began to provide unrationed meals for the children. Unfortunately, although I, personally, never took advantage of it, there was undoubtedly a widespread Black Market in all rationed goods. Quite early on, private motoring was banned, petrol only being available to such people as doctors on duty and other special categories.

While on the subject of food, it was quite interesting, and somewhat revealing, to observe how various people reacted to their rations of, in particular, confectionery and other little luxuries. In other words, those with, perhaps, a more reckless and happy-go-lucky nature, seemed to spend all their allocation of coupons in one go and have a glorious gobble-up; while others, of a more cautious or moderate tendency, would eke their supplies out so as to be able to enjoy things little and often!

Reverting now to the year 1940, my diary records that on the 7th of August we cleared out our loft, following Government directions, in order to reduce the risk of damage by fire-bombs. At the same time, I was making as much jam as possible while sugar stocks were not too bad, and taking advantage of the summer fruits available. However, on the 15th, in the early evening, we

The old mill house at Thatcham.

experienced one of the worst air raids locally when there was a sudden attack on the Croydon Aerodrome. It so happened that Dennis had arranged an emergency appointment straight from the office with his dentist for the extraction of two impacted wisdom teeth. On the way home he noticed a number of aircraft strangely manoeuvering in the direction of the aerodrome, and saw a column of smoke rising into the air. As he reached our front door the sirens sounded, and we realised that this was, in fact, a raid on the aerodrome and the adjoining factories. This was not exactly the best kind of treatment for one in his state, and he suffered very considerable pain all that night and was unable to move his lower jaw for some days to follow.

The next day there were a few more air raid warnings, but, by the Saturday, things seemed fairly quiet, and we decided to go ahead with our plans for a week's holiday at Thatcham in Berkshire. We travelled by coach and eventually arrived at a lovely old mill house in the depths of the countryside outside Newbury. We enjoyed the company of one or two other visitors in the house, and revelled in the excellent meals provided, especially the large bowls of thick cream, served with home-grown greengages and such-like. We sunbathed by the river, or sat in the garden and read,

21

or took photographs of the charming surroundings. In fact, the only nasty experience was at lunch-time on the day of our return, when, out of the blue, literally, a single enemy aircraft dive-bombed a nearby Army supply depot which we had not known was there. Needless to say, the sudden explosion was very unnerving, and we were quite glad to return to our own home in safety later that night.

During the last week of August, my diary records that we had an ever-increasing number of air raid warnings, day and night, and it was later realised that this was the commencement of the German air attack on south-east England; to become known eventually as The Battle of Britain. This situation involved our spending many nights in the Anderson shelter in our little back garden, so I will try to describe what this was like. We had a small mattress with various cushions and rugs spread all over the floor, so that we could sit or lie fairly comfortably; and, as it was not advisable to undress, we were able to keep warm (though as the autumn nights approached we managed to plug in a small electric bowl-fire). We also installed a hurricane lamp and a radiator lamp, which helped to keep the place dry, especially during wet weather. Dusk fell early by this time, and the night raids grew longer; so, as soon as we had managed to eat a quick evening meal, we would collect together our thermos flasks and biscuits, etc., ready to make a dash to the shelter as soon as the warning sirens sounded. My diary records that 'all the staff were half-awake so the office closed at four o'clock' — but, strangely enough, as we got used to things more, we managed to sleep quite well in our underground cave, once the all-clear had sounded and things went quiet for a few hours towards dawn. It must be remembered that all this took place years before it was the custom to do much in the way of camping holidays, and to use sleeping-bags and so on; hence it was all very alien to our normal way of life; to say nothing of the constant nervous strain of wondering whether it was 'one of our planes, or one of theirs' and if one of the bombs would have our name on it, as the saying went.

On September the 6th, I managed to get to the hairdressers in-between warnings, and on the 7th we had our lunch out, as it was difficult to cook meals with so many interruptions by raids; but

A painting by Frank Dickinson of the bomb damage in Carshalton High Street on the 7th September 1940. (This picture is on view in Little Holland House, Carshalton, where the artist lived).

that night we heard distant gunfire, and saw flames when there were dreadful raids on the London docks; and many bombs also dropped locally, especially in Carshalton, when part of the hundred-and-fifty-years-old butcher's shop, Haydon's, was wrecked. (There had been a butcher's shop there for about 300 years.) This and later damage eventually led to the whole of the premises having to be demolished. The same bomb destroyed the two-hundred-years (or more)-old King's Arms inn on the opposite side of the High Street. Even closer to our own home were the bombs which fell later that week in Lodge Road and Ross Parade, with their thunderous crump, out of the blue, only a few minutes away.

During these dangerous and difficult weeks one can trace the beginnings of the famous slogan 'Business as usual', when it became a point of honour, so to speak, to try to carry on life and work as normally as possible, despite the trials and tribulations of the blitz. Among the unsung heroes of those days were the men and women who continued to travel daily to their places of work, often in various parts of London, in order to keep the business

23

side of the country running, and to staff shops, offices, canteens, hospitals, and so on. My father was one of these who had to brave the train journeys to London and back every day, despite frequent air raid warnings; and after his day's work he would take his turn at the Wardens' Post, in the evening or night.

And here, for the benefit of those readers who did not live through those years, I will explain briefly what that was all about. Throughout the entire country, every town and village was subdivided into groups of roads, and special brick-built Wardens' Posts were erected (blast-proof, it was hoped) to be manned night and day by a mixture of paid personnel and volunteers, working on rotas; men and women alike, who were not required for active service. They were in constant touch by telephone with the main Report Centre (usually in the basement of the local Town Hall, or the like) who, in turn, would call out the Auxiliary Fire Service, or ambulances, when required. This Air Raid Precautions organisation soon became well-known as the A.R.P. The wardens were issued with light-weight steel helmets, special gas-masks, and, later, a dark-blue battledress type of uniform. I think they also had handbells and rattles for use in warning people of dangers. In the Wardens' Posts would be pails of sand, stirrup-pumps, and first-aid equipment, for use in minor incidents; but their main duties were, during a raid, to report incidents; to patrol the streets; and also check that all premises were completely blacked-out so as to give no help to enemy aircraft overhead. They subsequently became known as the Civil Defence Service.

As the weeks lengthened into months, and the months into years, a great camaraderie developed among these brave folk — and, dare I say it, quite a few romances blossomed, and occasional jealousies among married couples. This I know for a fact, as my own mother always suspected my father of 'getting up to mischief' when he went round to the Post as the bombs began to fall!

In addition to the A.R.P., many firms had their own volunteer roof-spotters on the watch, and the Observer Corps were active out in the fields in country districts, helping to plot the approach of enemy planes. And, of course, one need hardly mention the legendary Home Guard, years later to become known to so many through the television series 'Dad's Army'.

24

The local Home Guard marching up Woodcote Road, Wallington. Note the anti-blast tape on the windows of the shop on the far right, (Edith Kay).

Reverting now to a more personal note, in the third week of that September my husband received notice to attend his medical examination, prior to call-up, in order to decide what category and service he would be put in; so we felt very miserable at this prospect, to say nothing of coping with air raids or warnings day and night, still. A few days later, Dennis was told he would go into the Royal Air Force, as a member of the ground staff, his bad sight precluding him from flying duties. But we knew it could only be a matter of weeks before he would be called up, so we had to begin making plans for that period and try to decide the best thing for me to do.

Meanwhile, about this time, my father-in-law heard that, in common with many others, his Department of the Ministry of Health, was to be moved from Whitehall in London to the West Lancashire coastal resort of Blackpool (of which more anon) so it was felt that the wisest thing was for me to join them there once Dennis had actually joined the R.A.F. This, of course, in turn, meant that we would have to give up our flat and store our furniture 'for the duration', as it was our hope that, once my husband had completed his initial training, I would be allowed to join him wherever he was posted (in Great Britain) so that he could live 'out of camp' in whatever furnished lodgings we could find.

So it came about that, during the month of October (in between daily air raids or warnings) we began gradually to pack up things like our china and glass, ready for storage. On the 14th three bombs fell very close to us in nearby Tharp Road; and Dennis received orders to report to Bedford on the 19th for 'deferred service'. This would take up most of the week-end; so, after an early start in order to get him off by hired car to the London train terminus, I took myself off to my parents' home in Park Lane, Wallington, to pass the time there. As it happened, the station in question had been put out of action in the previous night's raid, which involved another journey to a different station in order to pick up the train for Bedford. The object of the exercise was for him actually to be enrolled officially in the R.A.F., and then to be placed on 'deferred service' until required. Needless to say, as it was the weekend, no action was taken until the Monday! He duly returned late that evening after a long and, because of damaged railway lines, trying journey.

Meanwhile, I had spent quite a jolly time with my parents and sisters, despite the fact that we had to spend every night deep down in our spacious cellar-shelter and sleep on the newly-installed bunks. In those days many houses had large cellars built under them; and, in the case of The Myrtles in Park Lane, we had ample space for several people and were able to spread ourselves out and sit in deck chairs, etc. The only one missing from the family circle was our faithful maid-of-all-work, Jenny, who had a horror of being buried alive under the rubble if the house had a direct hit; and so preferred to go on sleeping upstairs in her little front room, despite our pleas to make her change her mind. During that weekend more bombs fell nearby in Milton Road, Wallington; and also in Carshalton, finally wrecking the ancient premises of Haydon's, the Butchers.

A week later, on October 26th, we spent a miserable day supervising the removal of all our lovely new furniture and belongings to the now empty house of my in-laws in Ashcombe Road, Carshalton (they having been evacuated to Blackpool) where it was to be stored 'for the duration' — a phrase new to us at the

Carshalton High Street around the turn of the century. Haydon's, the butcher's shop, is on the right, behind the trees. A delivery cart with the owner's name can be seen on the left.

The cellar at The Myrtles, Park Lane, Wallington, converted into an air-raid shelter.
Above: The author's mother.
Left: The author (left) with her two sisters, preparing to spend the night in the cellar shelter.

28

time, but one that we had to get used to hearing for the next five years. Dennis and I spent the week-end clearing up everything at our flat and finally took ourselves off to my parents' home in Park Lane, where we were to stay pending his actual call-up. Air raids and warnings were still continuing intermittently day and night, so most of our evenings were spent *en famille* down in the cellar-shelter, but we had a good few laughs in between times, and my diary records that I even bought a new grey felt hat one Saturday during a brief shopping excursion to Sutton! In those days November 11th was still observed as Armistice Day no matter which day of the week it fell on – but my diary says 'No proper Armistice Day – just raids instead'. On a lighter note I also recorded that on the 27th I 'wore pyjamas for first time again' as we had not dared to undress properly all those weeks since the raids first began. I also 'bought ten shillings' worth of toilet items for storing' – now about ten pound's worth.

By this time we were managing to visit the cinema now and again when there were no raids on, but most of the time, right up to the end of December, the bombs still fell in one part of London or another. Then, on the 21st, my husband finally received his call-up papers to report back to the R.A.F. station at Cardington in Bedfordshire on the 2nd of January, 1941: so, this was the crunch, and I had to hand in my resignation at the office, as our plan was for both of us to travel up to Blackpool to join my in-laws for Christmas; and then for Dennis to travel to Bedford later, as instructed. It was a cold and damp day when we left Wallington on the following Tuesday at 8.30 a.m., and a memorable journey was experienced, as the train was three hours late in arriving; in typical war-time fashion! Somehow we managed to secure seats, despite the carriages and corridors being crammed to overflowing with travellers of all kinds (service and civilian). The fact that, between us, we ourselves had about thirteen pieces of luggage, did not help matters; but we did manage to obtain some lunch on the train. Never having been to Blackpool before, we alighted at the wrong station (South Shore), having been told that this was the nearest for our destination; but this was incorrect as we should have gone on to the Central Station. Luckily, we were able to pick up a taxi in spite of the late hour, and we finally reached the hotel where we were to stay with my in-laws who were billetted there.

After a meal we were so tired that we more or less fell into bed, and this was to be our first raid-free night's sleep for many months past. What bliss! The Christmas holiday was passed in peace and comfort, with plenty of extra goodies to eat; and we were able to enjoy several walks along the sea-front and benefit by the fresh air after so many hours spent in shelters. On Monday the 30th we even went to a traditional pantomime, *Dick Whittington*, and attended a New Year's Eve dance at the Grand Hotel; so we lived out the closing hours of this momentous year in style, despite the sadness of our approaching separation and the dreadful uncertainty of the future. For the record, in 67 nights in succession, 40,000 Londoners were killed or injured in one year.

Bomb damage in Beddington Gardens, Wallington, January 9th 1941.

CHAPTER FOUR: 1941

Before embarking on the next part of my narrative, I feel I should explain that the move to Blackpool really constituted a major change in my whole life and outlook. To understand this, I must further explain that, hitherto, my experience of people and places had been mainly restricted to my home town in the outer London suburbs and our annual holidays to various resorts along the South Coast, and, later, to Somerset and Cornwall. In those far-off days it really was a major expedition to venture even into the other London suburbs, especially across the river; and, in fact, this seldom arose, since all one's relatives and friends seemed to live near enough to visit easily and quickly. Also, of course, neither my husband nor I had ever had to live in lodgings, apart from holiday guest-houses or hotels; so the total experience came as a very great and sometimes unpleasant ordeal. Thus the way of life; the climate and scenery; even the food and transport, of Lancashire, were quite novel to us all. It may also be necessary to point out, for the benefit of younger readers, that the reason for choosing places such as the west coast of Lancashire was that they were much further away from the expected German air attacks across the English Channel; although, of course, industrial targets such as Liverpool were always at risk and suffered numerous raids.

It was, therefore, a wonderful thing for us to find life much more normal after the harrowing times of the past summer and autumn; and to sleep quietly in proper beds, with only a very occasional Alert to disturb one. This is not to forget that we had left behind all our closest relatives and friends, many of whom had to continue living in those vulnerable and dangerous areas for the rest of the war, and had to endure the later dreaded flying-bombs and V-2s (rockets). There was thus a constant anxiety about what was happening at home, as of course there were only the scantiest details printed in the daily papers, owing to censorship. ·

The general war-time upheaval resulted in the break-up of much family life, and scattering of friends. Certain categories of women

31

and girls were exempt from national service: i.e. expectant mothers, women with children, and, of course, the elderly. The wives of military personnel were not liable to call-up in the armed services, but were directed to work in factories, Civil Defence, Auxiliary Police, etc. One such was my sister Joan, whose young husband was a Territorial (soldier), who was captured by the Italians in North Africa and spent several years as a prisoner-of-war in Italy and Germany. She chose the local Police Force and continued to live in her flat, having only been married for three months when the war broke out. One of my friends, who was a Civil Servant in the Ministry of Labour, obtained a commission in the A.T.S. (now the Women's Royal Army Corps) and saw service in various parts of the country. My other sister, Peggy, was evacuated with the London office of the Ocean Insurance Company to a block of flats in Cheam Road, Sutton, and was 'Reserved'; but she also served as an Auxiliary Nurse in the local hospital in her spare time. In some cases various members of families were able to evacuate themselves privately to country districts; but most had to 'stay put'.

Returning now to January, 1941, it was frosty but sunny on the 1st when I saw my husband off on the train to Bedford to commence his war service, and I felt indeed very sad and somewhat lost at this our first real separation almost since we first met in 1936. We had made a promise to write several times a week whenever possible; and, sure enough, I received my first letter from him two days later. I print it here practically intact (leaving out a few endearments!) as it throws some interesting sidelights on those days:—

'Arrived here [R.A.F. Station Cardington] about 8.15 p.m., after a comfortable journey, but very slow — two hours late at Rugby — and had an hour's wait at Bletchley, but as it was in a coach it was quite nice and warm. I only had about a half-hour's wait at Preston, so I did quite well on the whole [he had left Blackpool at 10.10 a.m.!]. Met several nice R.A.F. men in the train to Bedford, and an older one took me in hand, as it were, and came along in the bus to Cardington. Have just had tea and cakes in the canteen, and have made my bed, so all is well for tonight. The warning went as I landed in Bedford, and planes have

32

Above: The author's sister, Joan, as a member of the local Police Force.

Below: Left to right - Margaret Kimber (A.T.S. Officer); the author; and Margaret Honer (née Keslake).

33

passed over in the distance. We also had a warning all the way down to Warrington. It is snowing now but not too cold. We met the snow just outside Warrington. It made the country look lovely. I sat on the opposite side coming down and saw much nicer country than going up. Two or three old water mills like Thatcham, very pretty, also a lovely old stone bridge. You would have loved it. The airman who took me round the camp tells me I may go to Morecambe first, then to Cranwell for training for a five-weeks' course for Equipment Assistant. He tells me it is quite easy to get a sleeping-out pass and said it is the best way, so we may be together again quite soon.'

I felt a little more cheerful after reading this letter, despite the fact that I knew how much Dennis must be hating it all, as he had always been an essentially peaceful and home-loving type of young man; so all this would be quite alien to his nature. Added to everything else would be the unavoidable rough conditions and inferior food of service life, plus having to endure the company of people not of one's own choice or tastes; but, like everyone else, we would both put a brave face on it and count any blessings that came our way.

Meanwhile, I was able to enjoy my freedom from the office work of several years past, and took advantage of my leisure by walking along the seafront whenever weather allowed, having tea or coffee in the town's cafés with other wives of Civil Servants now at a loose end by being billetted-out instead of living in their own homes in the far-away South. I note that I began to notice the colder climate, and decided to start knitting some woollen cami-knickers and some long green woollen socks! Also in my diary I can see the beginnings of the friction and problems created by this billetting of people on unwilling hotels and landladies, who normally enjoyed several months of leisurely life after a hectic but very profitable summer season of visitors every year. They were now required to house and feed service personnel, or civil servants and their families, on what they considered to be very inadequate allowances from the Government. Most of the 'displaced' wives were middle-aged women who had been used to reigning supreme in their homes and who naturally found it very hard to have to share kitchens for such chores as washing and ironing, having rotas

34

for bathing, as well as sharing communal sitting-rooms. In the day-time, while their men-folk were at their offices, there was not much else for them to do except walk in the streets, and haunt the cafés for a sit-down and a cup of tea or coffee in the warm, as they were certainly not welcome to stay in their billets for hours on end and involve the maintenance of fires, etc. Thus, many adopted the custom of the residents, and began to drop in for a drink at the local public-house or hotel during the blacked-out evenings, and chat over the day's problems with their husbands (and many, to my knowledge, had never been in the habit of drinking at all, in contrast to today's free use by women of clubs and pubs). It slowly became obvious to me that provincial life was quite different from the very enclosed life I had been used to in the London suburbs, and that quite a lot of prejudice existed between 'North' and 'South' — some justified, some not. Many women were desperately frustrated at the loss of their home-life and housekeeping; at the same time being too old for war work. Thus, as time went on, the great aim was to rent a small furnished flat and try to achieve a more normal way of life. My mother-in-law was one of those who suffered great unhappiness through the loss of her home and garden, and never really recovered, though she was, of course, thankful to be free of the air raids.

Blackpool as a town, I, personally, found quite satisfactory, with its plentiful shops, cinemas and theatres; although it possessed very little natural beauty or landscape as compared with the resorts I had known on the South Coast and in the West Country. However, I did notice that the general furnishings of the houses and hotels were of a good standard, particularly in things like velvet curtains, which were much thicker than the more flimsy curtains of net or cotton we were used to in the warmer south. Coal fires were very well made up (due, doubtless, to fuel being cheaper because nearer to the coal-mines); and windows, doors shop-fronts had to be really draught-proof owing to the intensity of the westerly gales which were often experienced. It was quite a common sight to see people bent nearly double while trying to cross to and from the sea-front at such times, and it was a regular occurrence for windows to be blown out if facing the promenade. Another curious fact I recall is that, for reasons which I never

Top left: Tram in service at Blackpool during the War.
Top right: On leave in Blackpool, Eileen and Dennis Whiteing.
Below: Blackpool, like many seaside towns, had defensive positions, or 'pill-boxes' built along the sea-front. Here, a pill-box on the North Promenade, is being demolished after the war.

understood, the sea never really smelt like the salty, seaweedy sea-air I had always known.

I was also very intrigued by the famous Blackpool trams which ran very frequently all along the front, and which were completely enclosed (unlike the London transport I was used to which were open at the ends). In many places they ran along a separate track, like a railway, and not part of the road, as was usual. The famous cinema organist, Reginald Dixon, had joined the R.A.F., but was still installed at the Tower Ballroom, where he continued to entertain the visitors and the Forces with his memorable repertoire.

In the middle of January I received a letter from Dennis inviting me to spend a week-end at Morecambe where he had been sent for initial training and 'square-bashing' as it became known. I was very excited at the prospect, and thoroughly enjoyed the journey there by the country bus service via Lancaster, as it was all new territory to me, and I fell in love with the stone walls and unspoilt landscape. Actually, I think this was probably the first real journey I had ever undertaken alone in my life up till then, as I had always previously travelled with my family or friends, or latterly with my husband! Eventually I arrived at Morecambe and found my way to the hotel where he was billeted — only to find him very tired and fed-up, as he had that day again been inoculated (routine service measure) and had to stay indoors all that week-end . . . . However, we made the most of the brief time together and tried to cheer each other up with the promise of a further week-end visit the following Thursday. In fact, by then Dennis was much better and we were able to go along to the R.A.F. dance held on the pier.

Despite the arrival of frost and snow during the days that followed we enjoyed several walks and visits to the cinema, but the highlight was a meal we had at a little place called the Don Café, and which I have never forgotten. We only had eggs and chips, followed by tinned peaches and cream — but in those days it was already a luxury to have such things off the ration. I had begun to notice that in Blackpool (and later in Manchester) we were able to obtain various little 'extras' in the food line as compared with when we were in the London area — probably because of their proximity to the docks on the western seaboard where cargoes from America and other countries seemed to arrive safely. The gales and snow became much worse by the Monday so that there were no buses for my return journey and I was obliged to come back by train. As will be imagined, poor Dennis had a terrible few weeks of outdoor drill in the icy snow, mostly in the car park behind the Winter Gardens on the sea front! And getting used to service boots proved a real nightmare. No wonder that when I next visited him he had to spend most of the time in bed with a severe sore throat and cold, plus neuralgia in his head. Oh dear!

I was able to visit Morecambe twice more, and then Dennis came back to stay with us at Blackpool for seven days' leave before being posted to his next camp; so we were able to enjoy being together and went to several cinemas and theatres. And here I should point out that, during the entire period of that war, great stress and priority were given by the authorities to the value of entertainment in all its aspects, in maintaining the general morale and mental stability of the forces and the civil population. Hence, wherever possible, the cinemas and theatres were encouraged to stay open, and many new spheres of live entertainment and recorded music were introduced to factories and canteens, such as *Music while you Work, Workers Playtime,* and so on — apart of course from the endless stream of shows put on for the forces by ENSA and others, where amateurs and professionals often appeared together; the latter often being classed as Reserved because of their value in that specialised field.

At the end of his leave, Dennis was posted to the R.A.F. Equipment Training Depot at Cranwell near Lincoln, so once more he boarded the train and I resumed my daily life. During those weeks, my in-laws had made friends with one of the young Polish pilots who were stationed at Blackpool (having escaped from their own country to carry on the fight against Hitler), and we often met up with Henryk or invited him round to our billet in the evenings for a cup of coffee by the fireside, to cheer him up. Language difficulties were soon overcome and the Polish airmen proved to be very popular in general, largely on account of their extremely good manners and happy natures. About this time, my diary also records that there was a good deal of trouble and friction with our landlady over such domestic problems as missing

The Winter Gardens, Morecambe, c.1940.

Henryk, a Polish airman stationed at Blackpool who became a family friend.

laundry, bath rotas being ignored, and so on. Bearing in mind that most of us had never known what it was like to be in lodgings at all, it is not surprising that this sort of thing often happened.

I was therefore very pleased when Dennis wrote to suggest that I might go to Lincoln for a week-end at the beginning of March, and I still recall with great pleasure the lovely time we spent there in a really comfortable hotel recommended to us by a family friend. There was a wonderful feather mattress on the huge bed, and I remember hot water being brought up to us in copper jugs by a really old-fashioned maid. The meals were delicious, too, especially porridge served with fresh cream (country districts scored in this way)! Above all, literally, was the view of the magnificent cathedral rising up in the misty sunlight. Dennis seemed much happier, too, so I returned to Blackpool on the Monday feeling more cheerful, particularly as we were now to be installed in a new hotel, The Braemar, on the sea-front. I could not at this stage take up any specific war work as I was still waiting to hear where Dennis would finally be posted at the end of his training, in the hope that I could join him. Eventually, after another brief leave, the news came through at the beginning of April that he was to report to Cambridge — which seemed a wonderful place to be going to and better than we had feared. And so I began to make plans for packing up my bits and pieces once more in readiness for a message to say he had been able to find lodgings for us there; and sure enough I received a telegram on the 23rd April to say O.K., and I said goodbye to Blackpool and departed by train on Saturday the 26th for the next stage in our war-time life.

Cambridge to me is one of those special places, like Paris, that one either loves or hates, and in my case I fell instantly in love with the whole idyllic atmosphere of 'town and gown' — as witness the first entry in my diary 'very lovely old town but awfully quaint houses!'. The latter phrase became uncomfortably true for me all too soon once we were installed in our temporary lodgings in Botolph Lane, (near St. Botolph's Church) in an extremely old and ill-equipped house which possessed no proper kitchen or bathroom. The plan was that we should share the accommodation with another couple and their small boy, the

Above: By the River Cam.
Below: The Author outside the house in St. Botolph's Lane, Cambridge.

husband being Reserved on account of his work for a religious organisation. In the event, our time there was made extremely difficult and unhappy by the wife's neurotic state and all the attendant problems of trying to cope with the primitive domestic facilities. For someone like me, who had never had to 'rough it', I felt I had certainly been thrown in at the deep end! Nowadays, so many young people live in bed-sitters and fend for themselves with the aid of launderettes and supermarket convenience foods that it probably does not come so hard to cope with adverse conditions.

Dennis had secured a living-out pass, which meant that he came home for all his meals, except when he was on the rota for guard duty at night. He finally managed to buy a very ancient bicycle (by now these were like gold dust) to get to and from Jesus College where he had been assigned to the Rations Store, which supplied food and clothing to the Initial Training Wing of the R.A.F. in Cambridge, where air crew spent their early weeks of instruction. It was all a far cry from his quiet office in the Town Hall at Wallington, and, of course, being rather inexperienced and naive, he was somewhat shocked at the fiddles, and tricks of the trade, that went on in certain quarters; but that is another story.

Meanwhile, I found great compensation in being able to explore the town and various college grounds; particularly enjoying walks by the riverside in King's, where the willows trailed their pale greenery among the daffodils in the spring sunshine. I sometimes took a book, and spent a pleasant afternoon in the fragrant garden of Clare College; as, at this time, certain colleges were still occupied by some undergraduates, while others had been requisitioned by the services. I also found great interest in the town's market, where there was a plentiful supply of non-rationed vegetables, and produce from the outlying farms and villages. Another pastime was having tea or coffee in one of the famous Cambridge restaurants, notably *The Copper Kettle* and *The Dorothy* which were great rendezvous at that time. Certain afternoons, too, I would go along to help at the R.A.F. Canteen, which was manned by volunteers (at this point there was no actual direction of labour). We were also lucky in that we had very few air raid warnings in that area; though night-bombing on London was still very heavy and frequent; thus we were still able to go to the cinemas in the evenings, and also to visit the Red Cross canteen for coffee and company.

I think I am right in saying that it was about the middle of 1941 when we were suddenly confronted with the unwelcome news of clothes rationing. This meant that literally every item of clothing, except hats, would have to be obtained by giving up coupons, and these were very limited in quantity. It also resulted in the introduction of what became known as Utility garments — in other words clothes designed with the utmost economy and simplicity in design and material. Actually, this was quite a good thing in many ways, as the basic designs were re-thought by top designers and did away with many of the fripperies of pre-war dresses and coats. Head-scarves became very popular as hats became more scarce and expensive, and the habit of wearing mourning seemed to vanish overnight, as no-one could afford black outfits on so few coupons. It was quite common for whole families to club together in order to help a prospective bride to buy a wedding dress; and, of course, the black market thrived more and more. Later, the American forces became extremely popular for their generosity in providing the newly-developed nylon stockings, which became like gold dust in the absence of our pre-war pure silk stockings! A new phrase: 'Make-do-and-mend' entered the vocabulary, as every piece of cloth became doubly precious; and it became a widespread custom to save every minute piece of paper, stationery and string to be used over and over again. We began recycling without even realising it!

And so spring drifted into a lovely hot summer, and we took advantage of every free week-end to explore the nearby countryside, as bus services were still quite good. I recall, especially, the Sundays when we took a picnic up to the woods on the old Roman road to Newmarket, and sat under the warm, scented haystacks in nearby fields. Another memorable occasion was the day we found our way to the famous village of Grantchester, immortalised by Rupert Brooke in his poem. It has been called 'the poets' village', because it has, in its time, played host to others such as Chaucer, Milton, Spenser, Tennyson, Dryden and Byron. Generation after generation of students has mused or studied

44

beneath the willow trees of the romantic Grantchester Meadows, beside the River Granta; others have punted up from Cambridge to sample the delicious pleasures of taking honey and cream teas in the Orchard Tea Gardens which began serving such delights way back in 1897. The clock to which Brooke refers in the final couplet of his Grantchester poem is that of the Parish Church of St. Andrew and St. Mary —

> Stands the Church clock at ten to three?
> And is there honey still for tea?

My other special memory of those Cambridge days is of attending Evensong in King's College Chapel, that magnificent piece of architecture so drenched in atmosphere and unique in its glorious setting of lawns and river. The dim interior was lit by candles in the choir stalls, and the singing was superb, then, as now. I found great spiritual consolation there during those months of war-time upheavals and difficulties.

Another cheering event was the week-end when my parents and sisters came to visit us and we had a brief family reunion and exchanged all the news. Petrol was now rationed, so such visits were likely to be very rare. By the beginning of June, Dennis became due for seven days' leave, so we decided to get away for a few days and chose a guest-house in the tiny village of Harrold in Bedfordshire. This turned out to be a delightful sixteenth-century vicarage, set in a real country garden by the river, and we enjoyed every moment of our stay there, making friends with the family who accommodated us so comfortably. We explored the ancient church, watched the village cricket match, and visited the town of Bedford; and every day was blessed with sunshine. We were truly sad when the day came for us to return to Cambridge, and to this day have remembered the happy time we spent there. For the record, we, like most people then, had no car; so all our journeyings were by train and bus — and even in war-time the services were far better than at the present.

During these weeks I had been searching hard to find more congenial lodgings for us — not made easy by the fact that it was not allowed for officers and airmen to share the same billets. However, at the beginning of July we had a stroke of luck, and were able to move into 17, Malcolm Street, and enjoy the luxury of having our own sitting-room and bedroom, with use of kitchen (in the basement!). The landlady had been used to catering for undergraduates in normal times and was a very pleasant and motherly soul; so we had a much more peaceful daily life from then on. It was quite hard work for me to cook our meals down below stairs and carry them up on a tray to our first-floor sitting-room, and then carry things back again for the washing-up; but I was already beginning to learn how to cope with such problems, and was so thankful to be in what seemed like a little home of our own again. I would enjoy the daily walk to the shops and market-place, breaking my trip to have an ice-cream in one of the many cafés adorned with such names as *The Eros*, *The Whim*, *The Friar House* and so on. Sometimes, if Dennis had a little time off, he would row us along The Backs, or we would go on a visit to Ely and gaze with delight at the cathedral rising above the Fens. Another lasting memory is of the sound of music drifting through open windows while an undergraduate was playing the piano. So the summer passed into early autumn, and in the middle of September we spent a week-end leave back home in Wallington, where we crammed many visits to friends and relations into a few hours. My diary records 'lovely hot bath!' in appreciation of some real home comforts after the primitive conditions I had lately experienced. Later that month we travelled back to Blackpool for a further brief leave, leaving Cambridge at 6 p.m. on a Friday evening and arriving at Blackpool at 5 a.m. so as to make the most of each day's holiday with our in-laws and get up to date with their news. Apparently there had been further trouble in their billets, and they had made yet another move, always hoping for something better to emerge.

October held the usual autumn mixture of weather; and life jogged on uneventfully – until the very end, when, on the 31st, we learned that Dennis had been posted to Manchester, where he was to take up his duties two days later! That week-end was spent in feverishly packing up our various clothes and belongings into suitcases once again, taking a sad farewell of beautiful Cambridge, and catching a train on Sunday to take us up to Lancashire for the next phase of our travels.

Dennis had been posted to the R.A.F. station in Heaton Park, a

The Friendship Tavern, Prestwich, before the Second World War.

suburb of Manchester; but the nearest our taxi-driver could take us was to Prestwich, an adjoining district, where, through his kindly help, we were able to find accommodation for that night at *The Friendship* inn. Next day Dennis had to report to his unit, and I remember feeling very lost and desolate in this strange new town. However, we did have one contact in the shape of an R.A.F. colleague and his wife (recently married while in Cambridge), now also at Heaton Park; so I managed to find their lodgings and they kindly invited me to stay the week with them while I searched for a place of our own. This proved to be much easier than expected, for, within a day or two, I had located a council house whose tenants had been called up and obliged to move out, but who wished to let the house furnished. It was wonderful for us to be in a home of our own once again, and we soon settled down to a pleasant routine, with Dennis cycling to and from Heaton Park (all personnel had to 'live out' as there was no proper camp accommodation); while I enjoyed the company of my one friend there, Joan Sutton (the wife of Dennis's R.A.F. colleague), when we went out shopping together and explored the neighbourhood. As will be imagined, it was a dramatic change for me to be living in such a large city as Manchester — and little did I dream that I would be still there three years or so later! One was always haunted by the spectre of overseas postings, and could only live one day at a time, never banking on the future.

It was about this time that I had to register for 'direction of labour' purposes; but, as the wife of a serving airman, I was not eligible for call-up to the services. I therefore undertook to busy myself in voluntary work, and to this end went to the local headquarters of the Women's Voluntary Services (W.V.S., now Royal W.V.S.) to offer my knowledge of shorthand and typing, and to help with any other work I could do. I shall always remember with gratitude and affection the kindly welcome the ladies there gave me. Headed by Mrs. Paton-Williams (the wife of the Rector), Mrs. Bunbury, Mrs. Lambourne, and dear Miss Mills (a doctor's daughter in the old traditions of appearance and manner) we formed quite a good team, with other helpers, running a Sewing and Knitting Circle and distributing non-stop parcels of suitable warm garments and other comforts to every local man or woman now in the services, at home or abroad. From then on, most of my afternoons were fully occupied, and I began to feel a little more integrated with, and useful to, the war effort.

I found the climate of Manchester quite mild, though damp and misty, and, without exception, the people seemed so kind and friendly. On Dennis's days off, we were able to enjoy taking the bus into town to visit one of the many cinemas, or have tea out, or just enjoy window-shopping at the many big stores. Despite the black-out, the buses used to rush along at top speed, and we would hold our breath as we sailed home through Salford and finally landed safely in Prestwich! My diary records that 'we had a chicken and some extra goodies' for Christmas Day, which was made quite jolly for us by having Dennis's parents to stay for a week; so we finished 1941 in reasonably good shape, despite so many ups and downs.

CHAPTER FIVE: 1942

Reading again through the pages of my diary for 1942 I was amused to see that this little book contained in its preliminary pages a section entitled 'Household Law: Domestic Servants' which provided much useful information as to the engagement, dismissal and general treatment of servants — which only goes to prove that, even in the middle of the war, some things had not changed! The following pages contained a 'War-and-Peace Christmas Pudding' recipe, consisting mainly of grated raw carrot and potato, half a cupful of mixed dried fruit, and the same quantities of breadcrumbs and flour; but no sugar — a typical example of the horrible concoctions we had to invent in those days of drastic food rationing.

Our first winter in Manchester proved to be quite bearable, with frosty sunshiny days alternating with cold, damp ones; and, quite early in the month, we were able to travel down to Wallington for seven days' leave. I should, perhaps, make it clear at this point that everybody in the services, if stationed in Europe, was entitled to seven days' leave every three months, with free travelling passes; plus occasional 48-hour leaves in between; and these breaks were greatly looked forward to and savoured as times to see relatives and friends, many of whom were still enduring various kinds of air attacks from time to time.

Those early days of our life in Lancashire were brightened considerably by occasional visits from one of Dennis's R.A.F. comrades; namely, 'Dickie', otherwise known as Hugh Clifford-Wing, who loved to come to tea or spend an evening in our billet, entertaining us greatly with stories about life in London society, or the theatrical world which had been his métier before the war. He came from what is known as 'County' stock, and was charming and amusing, but not finding it easy to fit his artistic personality into the rough-and-tumble of R.A.F. life. After a while Dickie was allowed to organise entertainment for the Heaton Park camp, and, much later, he became manager of the No. 8 R.A.F. Gang Show organised by the legendary Ralph Reader.

By this time I was becoming quite familiar with the centre of Manchester, and would take the bus for a weekly trip to change library books, visit the hairdressers, or perhaps have tea at Kendal Milne's or Marshall's for a treat off the ration! Sunday evenings would find us quite often in St.Mary's Church, Prestwich, and occasionally there would be an R.A.F. dance to liven things up. Unfortunately, during March, we learned that the former tenants of our temporary home would be returning, having been posted nearer, so this meant yet another upheaval for us, and I was very depressed, as it was not easy to find lodgings with so many servicemen being billeted out. Eventually we moved into the house of a Miss Denny in Thorndyke Walk, where we once again had to share the kitchen; not an enviable situation.

During these weeks it had become obvious to all concerned that my friend, Joan, was expecting a baby; and this of course led to considerable problems, as she and her husband were in lodgings and had not planned to start a family so soon, having been married but a few months. But it must be remembered that, in those days, there was practically no contraception advice or help given, and this delightful couple were not only quite ignorant but deeply in love. It was very difficult indeed to find sufficient money or coupons to provide all the necessary baby clothes and items of equipment, and I was quite shattered at the makeshift cot and second-hand things that they were grateful for — though they did manage to buy a pram! Coming from a family background myself, where everything was conventional and 'up to standard', it was quite an eye-opener for me to see how people less fortunate had to cope.

As it turned out, during the ensuing months we were able to give Joan a good deal of support and company, as her husband Leonard was posted without warning to Lincoln and had to leave Joan behind until such time as he could find suitable accommodation for her and the baby. I can still picture Joan with her beautiful, East Anglian, true golden hair, blue eyes and fair skin and she give birth in early June to an equally lovely daughter, later christened Susan, in the local nursing-home (in those days this was quite usual). I used to enjoy going for walks with them during the summer weeks, or baby-sitting so that she might have an occasional outing to the cinema nearby — until the end of July, when she finally left to join her husband in Lincoln. After that, owing to the vicissitudes of war, we lost touch; and I often wonder what happened to that little family — and how they are faring now, all these years later.

During the late summer, Dennis and I spent a pleasant leave back home in Wallington, visiting family and friends, and even getting our bicycles out of storage so that we might cycle along the peaceful Surrey lanes, through Chipstead and Banstead, with tea at Dene Farm, our favourite haunt in pre-war days, when cream teas in the garden in summer, and enormous log fires in winter, added to the pleasant atmosphere of the old-world setting. This must have been a fairly quiet time as regards air raid alerts, though my diary does record quite a few of these shortly after our return to Manchester in August. Germany was busy bombing Russia by now.

Most days I was able to continue with my work at the W.V.S. centre; but on Saturdays or Sundays, when the weather was fine, I was able to enjoy, though the great kindness of Mrs. Bunbury, one of the organisers, the sun and seclusion of her garden, complete with a deck-chair. This was a real treat, as it was seldom possible to find lodgings with such facilities, and it was quite a hardship for me to be deprived of a garden for so many years.

September 11th proved to be quite a red-letter day, for it was then that we had yet another change of lodgings — this time into the accommodation vacated by Joan and Leonard, which was actually an upstairs sitting-room and bedroom over the grocer's shop owned by Mrs. Rothwell and her son Walter, both of whom proved to be kind and friendly folk — so much so that we spent almost two years in that house, right up to the time Dennis was posted overseas. The shop was situated in the main road of Prestwich, called Sedgeley Park, and so was quite lively for me when I was alone, and also very handy for the other shops and bus stops, as well as the cinema just across the street. I still recall the delectable sticky buns and other delights that were on sale (off the ration) at the cake-shop opposite, and were a great boon to me in those days, as my main facilities for cooking were a small gasgrill and rings on the landing, with occasional use of the oven in the downstairs kitchen; and most of my washing-up having to be done in the bathroom sink! There was only a small back-yard, and the coal had to be fetched up from the underground cellar — but the kind and peaceful atmosphere more than made up for such unavoidable difficulties; and at least we were 'on our own' in our little upstairs haven, and I tried hard to make it as homely as possible. The battery radio was one of our main sources of entertainment most evenings, though we did visit the cinema often and enjoyed the escapism it provided. By now I was getting quite hardened to coping with other people's cooking-pots, china, bedding and furniture — but it was not easy as I have always been by nature a domesticated and home-loving creature, and, having been married so shortly before war came, it was heart-breaking to pack away all my nice new household goods and chattels. But we reckoned it was worth all the effort and sacrifice, to stay together for as long as possible, not knowing if there would ever be any future.

Recalling that period, certains things stand out in my memory of domestic life: such as the helpful butcher who would try to see that we got a tiny joint once a week with our combined rations; and the occasional few extra eggs and a chicken kindly brought to me by a friend of my father's who lived in the outlying country area where farm products could sometimes be obtained more freely. A local gardener used to supply a bundle of super lettuces scented with sprigs of mint and parsley, plus a few spring onions thrown in! I was, of course, registered at Mrs. Rothwell's for the main grocery rations, but we maintained a strictly impartial relationship, and I did not expect to obtain extras because of living over the shop. There were, in those days, no such things as washing machines or spin-driers, and I had to share the use of a vacuum cleaner; and did all my ironing with an old-fashioned flat iron, as one could not be sure of electric points everywhere as in these days. Many years have passed since the time I am writing about, but we kept in touch with Mrs. Rothwell and Walter; and, although his mother is now dead, we have in fact had a visit from Walter and his son Andrew only this year and exchanged memories of those days.

A note in my diary for Sunday, November 15th 1942, records that 'church bells were rung for victory in Egypt' — a special occasion for rejoicing indeed, as church bells were forbidden to be rung up to that date, except to warn of imminent invasion. This entry ties up with another one in which I recorded saying goodbye to one of my oldest friends, Henry Haydon of Carshalton, when he was posted to an R.A.S.C. unit in North Africa. Being a master butcher (his family business dating back about three hundred years) he was (naturally!) put in charge of petrol supplies — similarly, one of my husband's friends who had been an oil executive was immediately put in charge of meat supplies! Those readers familiar with war-time days will recall that this sort of thing was a standing joke and always seemed inexplicable.

I seem to have ended this year in style, buying a camel-hair coat for £5 (about £100 now, I guess) and having my hair permed as a Christmas treat, in order to present a good appearance for the coming New Year.

CHAPTER SIX: 1943

Looking back I realise that 1943 turned out to be a very stable period for us — largely because Dennis made himself so efficient and reliable in his work at the Heaton Park unit that special efforts were made to ensure that he was retained for a year (this was made possible in certain special cases). It was during this year that we got into the habit of spending part of our quarterly leave in Wallington, in order to visit my family and our other relatives and friends; and then to travel direct up to Blackpool from London so that we might spend a few days with Dennis's parents (who incidentally were still changing billets every few months). My mind boggles now at the thought of so much travelling, often in cramped conditions, with long delays, as I have never enjoyed travelling as such, and , in fact, always suffered bad sickness as a child in cars or trains — but it is surprising what one can endure if circumstances make one really determined (and I do not recall any travel sickness tablets being available as they are today!).

During this time I began a regular weekly correspondence with my friend Henry Haydon, now posted to North Africa and later to Italy, and looked forward greatly to his always interesting replies. Special very thin air-graphs were available for use to the Forces overseas. I am sure that Major Haydon will not mind my recalling that I was one of the few people who could ever decipher his unique and extremely difficult handwriting! When in Wallington on leave we always made a point of visiting his wife, the former Rachel Cash, and their two baby daughters, who, together with Mrs. Haydon senior, were then living in Salisbury Road, Carshalton, following the bombing of their historic home in the High Street.

Very occasionally my father visited Manchester on business for his London office, and I looked forward to seeing him and being taken out for dinner at the Grand Hotel where he was staying. At a time when it was a red-letter day if we had poached eggs for supper, this was obviously a special treat in elegant surroundings.

Another note in my diary in the early spring records my delight at being able to buy a bunch of daffodils, since although, throughout the war, home-grown flowers were reasonably available for special occasions such as weddings and funerals, their prices had soared sky-high and turned them into an extravagance.

As mentioned earlier, citrus fruits from overseas had become unavailable so you can imagine my delight when I received a parcel of lemons from Henry Haydon in far-away North Africa — a gift which I rapidly transformed into two pounds of marmalade, using my precious sugar ration. During these months I was still spending most afternoons working at the W.V.S. centre; typing, sewing bandages, packing up comforts and Christmas parcels for 'the boys and girls', and the general war effort was still plodding on, as the grand invasion of Europe had not yet taken place. We had one or two nasty scares about Dennis being posted overseas, but these turned out to be mistaken messages from headquarters, and we breathed again. I see that on our periodic leave in the London area we visited the legendary *Windmill* theatre which was earning its famous slogan of 'We Never Closed'. Compared with the current crude and over-permissive shows of this type, those revues were of a remarkably high standard of artistic approach and humour, and obviously contributed greatly to the morale of war-weary audiences enjoying an hour or two of escape from reality.

And so, yet another year drew to its close and we celebrated Christmas in Prestwich once again; but this time we had a special treat when we were invited to dinner on Christmas night at the charming home of Mrs. Lambourne, one of our W.V.S. organisers — a wonderful meal amid warm surroundings and kindly friends, and a gesture I still recall with gratitude. I wondered: where would we all be by the end of the next year?

CHAPTER SEVEN. 1944

The weather during January proved to be quite mild, though damp and dull; and nothing special happened until the 31st, when we learned that Dennis had been seconded to work at the A.C.R.C. unit in Regent's Park, London, for four or five weeks (the letters stood for Air Crew Report Centre, which was the unit to which future air crew reported initially). He was to help in conducting a complete stock-taking of all equipment on the station. We quickly decided that I might as well travel down with him and stay in Wallington for a week or two to save being on my own in Manchester all the time, so we rapidly packed our cases and left the next day, the 1st of February, on an early train for London. We parted company at Euston and I completed my journey alone to my parents' home.

During the days that followed I was able to visit some of my old friends who still lived in the district, and we even enjoyed one or two brief trips out in the car with saved-up petrol rations. My diary, however, records that we had several air raid alerts during the period, mostly at night.

Dennis, meanwhile, was having a fairly bearable time in London, being billetted in the luxury flats of Abbey Lodge adjoining Regent's Park. In spite of the somewhat difficult work he was involved with, he was able to enjoy quite a bit of enter-tainment during his off-duty evenings. Free tickets for many West End shows were available to services personnel stationed in London, from a kiosk in Trafalgar Square. He also met up with our friend Dickie again, who was now managing No. 8 Gang Show, and who gave a performance for the station prior to going overseas.

We eventually returned to Manchester and settled down to normal routine once more as the spring turned into early summer. My pleasure in the sunny warm days was, however, suddenly shattered by the news on May 13th that Dennis was to be posted overseas — exactly when, we did not know, but he would be given

Damage caused by long range missiles in Wallington, July 1944.
Above: Bernard Road. Below: Woodcote Road; note what appears to be the nose cone
of a V2 rocket, in the centre of the picture.

embarkation leave immediately. As will be imagined, we spent a very miserable week-end at the prospect of our coming separation; perhaps for ever, who knew? But we had to make plans quickly, and decided to follow our usual practice of spending part of our leave in Wallington and the rest in Blackpool, so that Dennis could say goodbye to his parents.

Quite soon after our return to Prestwich, on June 6th to be precise, came the most exciting news of the war so far; namely, that the long-awaited invasion of France had taken place, in maximum advance secrecy, on the coast of Normandy, and I see from my diary that I went to a special service at St. Ann's Church in Manchester some time during that day. Owing to the necessary censorship we could not learn many details of the good or bad news of military activity during the months that followed, but we did soon learn that, as a reprisal, the German bombing of London had started up again through the use of the dreaded Flying Bombs and Rocket Bombs (V1 and V2) which resulted in large numbers of people being killed or injured — largely because it proved impossible to give adequate warnings of these particular bombs. Meanwhile, we remained in Prestwich, still awaiting an actual date for Dennis's departure; and this we learned on June 22nd, but, of course, no idea as to where, because of security regulations. Thus it was that on July 5th (two days before my birthday and a week before his own) Dennis left for Morecambe on the first stage of his overseas posting — and I left for Blackpool to join his parents with whom I was to live during his absence. To say that I was smiling through my tears would not be strictly accurate, as I felt too heartbroken and fearful of what the future might hold; but perhaps the following two quotations written in the back of my diary reveal my thoughts and feelings more truly:—

> That thou, residing here, goes yet with me,
> And I, hence fleeting, here remain with thee.
> *(Shakespeare: Anthony and Cleopatra)*

> God keep you is my prayer
> God keep you in His care,
> God guide you back to me —
> With love unabating
> I shall be waiting
> When you come back to me *(verse from a ballad)*

During the following days we kept in touch by telephone and letter, and, quite unexpectedly, I was actually able to spend two days with Dennis in Morecambe while he was being kitted-out and innoculated prior to leaving for overseas from Liverpool. In the days that followed we speculated endlessly as to his exact destination. Then, out of the blue, on July 31st, I was overjoyed to receive a cable from Dennis in Freetown on the coast of West Africa, where I felt that although the risks and problems of the climate would be hard to endure, the actual dangers of warfare would be less than in many other places.

From the many subsequent letters that I received I was able gradually to piece together a general picture of the primitive place, and type of work, Dennis now had to cope with. After a short period in the R.A.F. Transit Camp, it was found that no ship was available, so the whole draft had to be flown in a Sunderland flying-boat to the R.A.F. station at Bathurst in The Gambia. This station operated flying-boat patrols north and south along the West Coast of Africa from Freetown to Dakar. The camp itself was composed of two sections, one being of the ordinary type of Nissen huts, and the other built more in the colonial style of wood and corrugated roofs.

The Gambia was, in fact, at that time, the poorest of all British colonies; and therefore there was very little local food available for the services. Virtually everything had to be imported, with the exception of meat, which was locally produced but which was quite uneatable owing to the coarseness of the fibres. The food, generally, was considered by the powers-that-be as some of the worst in any permanent Air Force station. From time to time efforts were made to improve things, but as far as I could gather, then and since, Dennis existed mainly on a diet of peanuts, chocolate, eggs, and occasional local fruits, such as bananas and mangoes in season, which could be purchased from the natives. The climate was fairly pleasant in the dry season, but extremely trying in the wet season, owing to the intense humidity. There was a cinema where films were shown quite regularly and there was also an occasional live E.N.S.A. show. The town, although very small and primitive, provided quite a lot of 'local colour' in the work of the silversmiths plying their trade outside their huts,

60

and the various stalls set up in the open Albert Market. Dennis went quite often to the Pro-Cathedral of St. Mary's, where he was quite surprised at the very high pitch of the singing by the African congregation. On one memorable occasion he was invited to dinner with the Bishop of The Gambia, which cheered him up considerably.

Meanwhile, as they say, back in Blackpool, I began another phase in my war-time life. On arrival there I found that my in-laws were in the throes of yet another move to fresh billets, so it was arranged that I should lodge temporarily with a Mrs. West and her brother in Warley Road. She was a motherly soul and a very good cook, and I was lucky in being able to have a small sitting-room for my own use, including a typical roaring north-country fire when autumn arrived. Following an interview with the Ministry of Labour it was decided that I should commence work at the Ministry of Health offices which were evacuated from Whitehall; so on the 31st July I duly presented myself and entered into yet another of my war-time experiences — this time a very unhappy one.

To begin with, the offices were situated in one of the smaller hotels on the sea-front; and, being mainly a warren of tiny bedrooms and narrow passages, it was quite unsuitable for such purposes. Central heating was non-existent, the tiny bedrooms normally only being occupied by summer visitors; so we had to make do with small electric fires, or portable gas heaters, and wrap up as warmly as possible during the winter months. All the desks and chairs were makeshift, and the lighting equally poor. The stairs were very steep, and we had to take it in turns to descend twice daily to the antiquated and freezing cold basement to make the tea, with equally poor equipment, then carry the trays of thick chipped cups back up several flights (down again later to help with the washing-up!). Sanitation was, of course, also very limited, and unequal to the constant demands of a large staff of men and women.

I found the actual work very boring, and alien to my previous sphere; being the typing of a non-stop stream of replies dealing with insurance benefit claims, covering the entire country. We were always working about three or four months in arrears, owing to the shortage of man-power, and general war-time chaos. However, I could have coped with all this had the atmosphere been more pleasant. As it was, I found myself in a group of about five girls who had come over from Ireland as temporary typists, and who were extremely anti-British and hostile, as well as being lazy and disinterested. They seemed mainly to resent me because I spoke with a southern English accent and came 'from London'; and they gave me a very hard time in general, making no allowance for the fact that I was in a strange town, and that my husband was thousands of miles away and equally unhappy. Ireland being neutral, I suppose they had no personal involvement in the war as such, or sympathy for the likes of me. I had never come up against this kind of treatment before, and as I was a sensitive creature it made me very unhappy, though I tried hard to ignore many of the comments aimed at me. Small wonder that in the early autumn I fell quite ill with influenza and the doctor kept me off work for three weeks. The only bright spots in the depression that followed were the letters I received weekly from Dennis, and an unexpected visit from his aunt and uncle from London who had come up to say goodbye to their son, Raymond, who had joined the R.A.F. and now been posted overseas, via Morecambe and Liverpool.

So the year's end drew near and Christmas presents and plans had to be thought of; but unexpectedly my in-laws had the offer of a self-contained upstairs flat in Argyll Road (these were very scarce indeed) for renting, with two bedrooms included, and as my landlady was not too well at that time it was decided that I should move in with them and share expenses and housekeeping, to our mutual advantage, it was to be hoped. With a great scramble we managed to get ourselves moved, and installed in the new accommodation, two days before Christmas; and enjoyed the novelty of a kitchen to ourselves to cook a few extra goodies for the festive season, wondering all the time how poor Dennis was faring and how long it might be before we would all be together again.

CHAPTER EIGHT: 1945

This was to prove a momentous year, bringing victory and peace; but during the winter months and early spring one could not foresee this, and I was experiencing quite a lot of personal loneliness and depression, despite the fact (indeed, largely because of it) that I was now living with Dennis's parents in the long-awaited flat, which, although it helped to lessen many of the problems we had all endured, tended to increase daily tensions and friction. Without being disloyal, I feel it is only fair to explain that my mother-in-law had never been able to reconcile herself to the fact of the war as such, taking it as a kind of personal insult and unbearable burden — made now all the worse by the sending of her only child overseas. No doubt the tragic plane crash on her home, as described in an earlier chapter, had a devastating effect on her nerves, so that this, coupled with the years of living in billets with difficult landladies and colleagues, began to take a toll on her health, resulting in severe bronchial asthma attacks and general depression.

I was, of course, going daily to the Ministry of Health; but tried to help with housework and cooking when possible, and my evenings were often taken up with writing letters to Dennis and my friends overseas. There was also plenty of mending and patching to do, to make one's clothes last. Incidentally, at the beginning of my diary for 1945, I find a pencilled list of my clothing coupons budget as follows:—

Dress	6
Blouse	4
Shoes	7
Summer Dress	7
Winter Coat	18
Wool Jumper	6
Total	48

Total 48 with just a few spares left.

The house in Argyll Road, Blackpool, where the author shared a flat with her husband's parents.

My main diversion at this time was a trip to one of the many cinemas on a Saturday afternoon, on my own because my in-laws did not like films; or sometimes I would just walk round the town, window-shopping, and have tea out. Our friend, Walter, from Prestwich, would occasionally come over for a day during the weekend and we would enjoy some walks along the cliffs, and sometimes Mrs. Rothwell would kindly invite me to stay with them in our old flat, from whence I would re-visit my W.V.S. friends in Prestwich. One thing I never neglected was to pay all my earnings straight into my Post Office account, as I was able to manage on Dennis's R.A.F. pay (wife's allowance) and the remainder that he got 'made up' from the Council back in

Wallington (this was voluntarily done in many places as allowed by the Government). Much later on this nest-egg was to be used as part of the deposit on our first house.

Red-letter days now begin to appear in the diary, as for instance April 28th when I learned that my sister Joan's husband, Peter, was at last safely back in England after being a prisoner-of-war for nearly six years. Two days later, on April 30th, there is the entry 'Mussolini shot' — to be followed on May 2nd by 'Hitler reported dead'! Then came the most dramatic news of all, on May 7th: 'Germany has surrendered!!' to be followed on May 8th by 'Showery but very warm — VE-Day at last! Went to church in evening for special service and listened in on radio to the celebrations.'

Most of my readers will, I am sure, know that the initials of VE Day meant Victory in Europe — leaving the Far East war still to be won. Actual dates and exact details of many of these happenings were not fully known by the general public until much later, and, of course, there was no instant television by satellite to flash such news round the world; so we mostly had to rely upon rumours and reports in the daily press or the radio. Also, the process of winding up the war effort and demobilising all the Forces would take many months, so there was no instant return to normality in all directions; and rationing and restrictions were to last for several years after hostilities ended.

For me, life went on as before, working at the office every day and making the most of the summer weather in the evenings and at weekends. I also spent two brief holidays down in Wallington and began to wonder how soon we might all be returning there. Meanwhile, enormous efforts were being made to win the Far East war and my diary records on the 15th August 'Japan has surrendered'. So VJ Day had arrived a good deal sooner than anticipated, and to be honest I do not think we all grasped at the time that it was due to the Atom Bomb having been dropped, so the overwhelming feelings were simply of relief. It was not until later that the full horrors of atomic war were seen and realised, and peple began to wish perhaps that such a thing had never been invented. One thing is certain — it is too late now to turn the clock back.

Early in September I began to hear from Dennis that he thought he might be on the way home fairly soon, now that the war really was over, and, in any case, the tour of duty in West Africa was a maximum of eighteen months on account of the climate. Nevertheless, I was surprised and delighted when, on September 20th, I had a phone call to say that he had arrived at Morecambe, having come by ship from Freetown. He actually reached Blackpool late on the 22nd, and I do not need to describe the relief and pleasure we all felt at our reunion. He had brought many souvenirs and presents for us, made by the natives in Bathurst, and appeared to be quite fit, though much thinner and tanned (the latter due partly to the special anti-malaria drug which turned the skin yellow!). I had saved up my annual leave in order that we might spend some time together, and after a few days' rest we took the train down to London and enjoyed a round of visits and outings. In early October, however, life returned to normal once more, with Dennis having to report back to Manchester, and me to the office, as it was still likely to be some time before he would be demobilised. It turned out that he was to be posted to a maintenance unit near Wilmslow in Cheshire, and we planned that I should try to join him there as soon as he could find lodgings for me.

So it turned out that by the 5th November I had given in my notice at the office, packed my belongings, and taken the train for yet another temporary home, this time in the village of Cheadle. We had found quite a comfortable small house owned by an elderly widow, Mrs. Cadman, and her married daughter, Edna, who were prepared to let us rent a sitting-room of our own, with a bedroom, and use of the kitchen, so Dennis was able to cycle to and from the unit and come back for meals. Our landlady was a kindly soul, but who was not very well, and never left the house in all the time we were there; in fact my main memory is of her and her daughter making endless pots of coffee to sustain them through the winter days and frequently inviting me to share a cup with them; but not literally, I hasten to add! I was quite glad to be free of the office and back to a taste of domesticity and cooking, and I enjoyed walking round the pleasant village to shop after my chores were done. I still recall the porches of many houses being wreathed in the brilliant yellow stars of winter jasmine during those dark winter months, and determined to plant this shrub when once we had a house of our own and a garden to plan. We certainly had a great deal to be thankful for by the time Christmas arrived and were content just to spend the day by the fireside with a few special treats to eat, and presents and cards from family and friends to unwrap and enjoy.

PART III: THE AFTERMATH

CHAPTER NINE: 1946

The winter months of 1946 were quite cold and wet, and I soon developed a troublesome cough following a severe cold, which kept me cooped up indoors and I began to feel very depressed and isolated, as I had no friends or relatives anywhere near, and the landlady and her daughter tended to 'keep themselves to themselves'. I began to have occasional attacks of faintness and dizziness, for which the usual tonic prescribed by the doctor did not seem to be the cure. Looking back I realise that these symptoms were the first signs of reaction to all the years of war-time anxieties, heralding my first experience of nervous exhaustion. In those days we knew little about the relative needs for vitamins in our diet; and the years of war-time rationing were beginning to have disastrous effects on certain aspects of health. Since Dennis's return from overseas, and the ending of the actual war, we were also, of course, in a constant state of uncertainty as to when he would actually be 'demobbed' (batches of service personnel were released according to their group number, which was determined by age and length of service).

Meanwhile, when spring eventually came, it proved to be very warm and sunny, so we were able to enjoy one or two brief spells of leave during March. Dennis's parents were by this time preparing to return to Wallington from their long evacuation, but, unfortunately, the owners of the house they had rented in Ashcombe Road (following the requisitioning of their home in Foresters Drive early in the war) now decided that they would require that house back again for their own use; so there was no alternative but for us to shift both the two lots of furniture stored there back to Foresters Drive, and all move in together. The original plan had been that Dennis and I should move into the Foresters Drive house on our own, while his parents remained in the other one, but this was not to be. By that time all properties were so scarce, through the bombing damage, and lack of all building during the war years, that, throughout the country, it

68

The last 'pre-fab' house to be built in the London area, at the St. Helier Estate, Carshalton. The Rt. Hon. Charles Key (centre), Minister of Works, has come to present the key to the tenant on 9th June, 1948.

Memories of Cornwall. Above: Polperro. Below: Looe

was becoming impossible to rent or buy flats or houses of any kind. Really urgent cases had to be rehoused in the pre-fabricated small dwellings erected by the local councils on behalf of the Government. Many houses never looked the same again, at least not for years, as it took ages for repairs and decorations to be done where the services had requisitioned them; also, all front gates and railings of iron-work had long since been taken away to aid the war effort, which left some of the best roads looking very derelict for a long time.

Finally, on April 11th, my diary records that Dennis had been given his release date, so we felt jubilant and began to make plans for our return home. The following Wednesday he had to travel to Cardington for his official demobilisation, complete with 'civvy street' outfit of either suit, or sports jacket and flannel trousers; shoes, socks, shirt and raincoat — plus hat if desired! He was back late the next day, and, in order that we might celebrate Easter with the family, we managed to leave by an early morning train on the day following, which was Good Friday. We went straight to the Foresters Drive house, tired out but so happy, and spent a lovely weekend, all together. 'Everywhere looks so beautiful' records my diary — my reaction as a bred and born Southerner after so many years in the North Country towns, where trees and gardens were not quite so plentiful.

It was usual for everyone to be given about six weeks' special release leave, and we certainly made the most of our days that spring, visiting various relatives, and certain friends, who had, by now, also returned from foreign parts, and were trying to pick up the threads again. I was still not feeling very well, so we decided to get right away on our own for two weeks, and booked up at an hotel in Looe on the Cornish coast. After a long train journey, we were rather depressed to find the weather showery and chilly to begin with; but later on it turned very sunny and hot, so that we were able to enjoy the beach and have some outings, though public transport was not very good. We did manage to visit Polperro, one of my favourite spots since childhood days, and had lobster salad for tea (obviously a treat as it is recorded in my diary!). During those days we had many talks and arguments as to our future plans, mainly trying to solve the housing problem. One thing was certain; namely, that Dennis would be returning to his job at the Town Hall, as it was the law that (wherever possible) employers were obliged to keep open the jobs of men who had been called to the Forces (a great improvement on the chaos resulting from the First World War policy of no safeguards in this direction).

Thus it was that, at long last, Dennis reported back for work on June 3rd, and I tried to fit in as best I could to the housework and cooking routine, with his parents in Foresters Drive, always with the underlying frustration and depression of having no prospect in view of achieving a home of our own, in the light of the desperate housing situation throughout the country. Not surprisingly perhaps, looking back, I experienced one of the most alarming happenings in my life that summer, when I had my first attack of migraine. I had set out on a hot morning to do some shopping, when, out of the blue, I realised that my vision was disappearing, and coloured lights were whirling across my eyes in strange shapes and patterns. I was very frightened, and thought I was going blind, as I had never heard of the symptoms of migraine (it was not much researched at that time). My heart began to pound, and my legs felt weak, but I managed to grope my way down the road to where, luckily, I knew the chemist's shop was; and I remember collapsing there and stammering out how I felt. They sat me on a chair, and gave me a sedative to drink, which calmed me down sufficiently to return home and arrange a visit to the doctor to find out what the trouble was. He was rather vague but prescribed a nerve tonic and told me not to worry! Ever since that day, however, I have been subject to attacks of this kind, followed by violent headaches; though luckily, as the years have gone by, the intervals have lengthened, and I now understand better the cause and effect of this very distressing condition. One of the worst aspects is the uncertainty and lack of warning of an attack, with the risk of losing self-confidence if some important activity is involved. Doubtless many readers will know that it is one more case of 'learning to live with it'!

On a lighter note, there were great national celebrations on Saturday, June 8th, when the official V-Day processions and events took place; and, during the summer days which followed,

The Town Hall Wallington, mentioned opposite, decorated for the Coronation of George VI in 1937. This was the A.R.P. Report Centre (see page 13).

Victory Parade in Wallington: the band is marching past the Duke's Head, Wallington Green. Note the sign on the lamp post still pointing the way to an air raid shelter.

Dennis and I got our bicycles out of store and enjoyed several picnics in the lovely Surrey haunts we had known for so many years. However, another bout of trouble and anxiety was looming ahead, unknown to us, when Dennis's father suddenly became ill during the middle part of July, and did not respond to the treatment prescribed by the doctor. By the end of the month he had been further investigated, and X-rays were taken of his lungs, resulting in a great shock for us all when we learned that he was, in fact, suffering from tuberculosis — at that time greatly dreaded, as there was no certain cure and very little treatment; in contrast to the improved prospects of today when drugs have almost wiped this disease out in many countries. The classic old treatment was a spartan régime of bed-rest and fresh air, often in a mountainous climate such as Switzerland, for the wealthy; but the hospital newly built at St. Helier, Carshalton, decided that my father-in-law would make better progress if nursed at home, with constant rest, good food and personal care; laced with a large dose of good luck, which together might result in a cure.

As can be imagined, this was to be yet another dreadful burden for my mother-in-law to endure, just as she was trying to recover from all the war-time upheavals, and it meant the total re-arrangement of our already tightly-packed house, so that the patient could have a bedroom to himself and live as isolated as possible from the rest of the family, as it was known that this disease could be transmitted quite easily. All his cooking and eating utensils had to be kept separate and disinfected, and Dennis and I now had to live and sleep in the downstairs drawing-room, with all our own home still packed tightly in store in the back bedroom upstairs! Oh dear, I do not enjoy trying to re-live those difficult weeks and months, as we were all in a state of depression and tension, and friction became inevitable. For the record, we never really found out just how Mr. Whiteing picked up this disease, except that his lungs had suffered as a result of illness in the First World War; but in fact he did make a recovery after about a year, though he was not well enough to return to his office in Whitehall and opted for a premature retirement, in the hope that he and his wife might enjoy a few more years in happiness together. Sadly, these years were all too brief, but that is another story.

That autumn my own health seemed to go downhill in a series of nervous disorders and I began to lose weight drastically. In those days I was already quite slim, but I was now down to seven stones, so I was somewhat alarmed at this state of affairs and was persuaded by my mother to consult her own doctor. He was very understanding and sympathetic, and after a long talk explained to me that I was literally on the edge of a breakdown, but that, with special efforts in various directions, I should be able to get back on course before too long. He prescribed extra milk for me (only obtainable with a doctor's certificate), also sun-ray treatment at the local clinic throughout the winter — and what a winter that proved to be, as I shall tell in my next chapter. My diary closes 1946 with a reference to the first complete Christmas family party for eight years and the hope 'that 1947 will be a happier year for us all'.

CHAPTER TEN: 1947

I notice in the front pages of my diary a pencilled note of the local bus services between Wallington, Croydon and Sutton: these were running at every ten minutes throughout the day and evening – in contrast to the depleted services we have come to accept at the time of writing. It was therefore very easy for us to visit friends or go to the cinemas round about, without benefit of private cars which were very few and far between at that time; and these outings certainly made welcome breaks for Dennis and me while we were having to cope with the difficult situation at his home. There was no spare accommodation for us to live in at my own parents' house, and the outlook seemed very bleak. This was not helped by the fact that several of my friends, and my two sisters, were by now re-settled and having babies – not that I begrudged them, but I did feel I was being left behind, especially as by this time I was well into my thirties.

Looking back, I can see now that a large part of my depression, and the feeling that I was a fish out of water, was due to the fact that, whereas for the first twenty-five years or so of my life I had always lived down in the real centre of Wallington near to all the shops, my church, and my family and friends; I was now pitchforked into an area of the district previously unknown to me. This may sound silly but it is true to say, I think, that the development of Wallington above Stafford Road (i.e., Foresters Drive, Buckingham Way, Alington Grove, and so on) had little relevance to the great majority of the 'old' residents whose life still centred round the Manor Road and Woodcote Road shops. In fact, until I met my future husband, I had never visited any house in that part of the district, and hardly knew they existed! It also became increasingly obvious that, in reality, life was never going to be the same as it was in 1939; because so many threads had been broken that could never be joined again. I am thinking especially of all our little local activities, so many of which had to be disbanded and never started up again. I estimate that, during the 1930s, there were, at least, the following tennis clubs all flourishing: Wallington Cricket and Tennis Club in Hillside Gardens; Beddington Lawn Tennis Club in Beddington Park; Bute Park Tennis Club in Osmond Gardens; a small club in Hawthorn Road; another small club in between Grosvenor Road and Taylor Road and Springfield Road; Purley Cricket Club in The Ridge; apart from public courts in the various parks. The upheavals of the war years resulted in so many people being scattered to new districts and livelihoods, that the old familiar life-style seemed sunk without trace.

As part of the cure for my poor health, it was decided now that I should try to find some part-time work — not easy to come by at that time in a small place like Wallington, with few offices or factories. However, I arranged an interview with my former employer, Mr. Ernest Hayes, founder of a local printing and publishing firm in Manor Road, Wallington, for whom I had worked for over ten years as secretary and editorial assistant before the war. It so happened that he was short-handed through some of his staff still being on war service, so he was pleased to offer me part-time office work straight away.

In early January, therefore, I began yet another phase of my life by going to that office every morning and joining Dennis for lunch in one of the local cafés. Unfortunately, that month (and indeed the two months following) saw the worst snow and ice that had been experienced in living memory. The pavements became death-traps with solidly packed frozen snow, day in and day out, resulting in many broken ankles and legs. Public transport also got into chaos, as it was impossible to keep up with gritting and snow-clearing, week after week. This added to my personal difficulties, as I now had to make my way on foot two after-noons every week to the Health Clinic in The Grange, London Road, Wallington, for the special sun-ray treatment ordered by the doctor; then trudge all the way home in the bitter weather.

Added to the snow, there was the problem of the worst fuel crisis the country had ever had, in the aftermath of war, so that frequently we had the electricity cut off completely for hours on end, spending our evenings by candlelight, and with no heat unless one had a kitchen boiler with coal. Central heating was hardly known then and coal was very short. Burst pipes were a wide-
78

spread occurrence, and post-war manpower difficulties made it very difficult to get repairs done. My February diary records 'Colder and darker than ever. No heat or light in the shops'. But on the 14th I managed to buy some snowdrops, and we had eggs and bacon for supper (obviously still a treat). Snow and blizzards dragged on into March, and the diary records 'Words fail me' . . . .

But, as always, the great thaw did eventually set in, and, by April, there was a promise of spring in the air and we even began to get the garden tidied up — this had always been Mr. Whiteing's pride and joy, full of roses and new fruit trees, but, during the war and the occupation by the R.A.F., it had become so neglected as to be a wilderness, especially since the illness of its owner, who had formerly spent all his leisure hours tending it. During these lighter evenings Dennis and I would go for a stroll round the nearby roads, or into Roundshaw Park at the far end of Foresters Drive. It was during one of these walks that we began to wonder whether Wates the builders would be allowed to complete the building of some new houses in Hamilton Way interrupted by the outbreak of war. Only six houses had been built out of a planned total of about two dozen, so we thought it might be worth investigating the prospects. As the result of a phone call, we were able to arrange an interview at the Norbury offices of the builders on May 6th, where we learned that licences were to be granted for the building of twenty-four houses, to be sold to people approved by the local Council as being in urgent need (all building had to be licensed on the basis of a ratio of about four by local authorities to one by private builders). Dennis's war service, plus my long residence in Wallington and the difficult circumstances in which we were now living, involving a health hazard, all added up to a good chance that we would be allowed to purchase one of the new houses, so we filled in all the necessary forms and went home in great delight, though we had to wait several weeks before we knew the result.

It was, in fact, on June 17th that we had a letter telling us that official permission had been given for us to buy one of the Wates houses, and it is hard to describe how utterly relieved and thrilled we both felt. Later on we would have to arrange the financial side, but luckily, with the money I had been saving from my earnings, plus an equal amount from Dennis, we knew there would be enough for the initial deposit and sufficient income to meet our monthly mortgage. The cost of the house in 1947 was £1,650 — in 1983 about £40,000. It proved to be a hot sunny summer for once, and we made the most of our weekends by visiting a sports and country club not far away, where we played badminton and tennis, cooling off with frequent dips in the swimming-pool in the grounds. The news of our house acted as the best of tonics for me; and although I was still extremely thin, I did begin to pick up generally, and also to look ahead. I see that the temperatures soared up to 87 and 90 degrees Fahrenheit, and I was kept busy in my spare time making jam and trying to sort out various domestic problems ready for our removal day. The fine dry weather was a great boon in the building of those houses, which began to grow at a cracking pace, and we spent many evenings just walking by and watching the progress! Because of land shortage generally, the design was to be for a three-storey, simple, semi-detached house, with an open-planned front garden, and a fairly narrow back garden.

During September we had several trips into Croydon to arrange for new curtains to be made (at Ebbutts), and on one red-letter day I managed to buy some oranges (obviously these were still very scarce). There was also the exciting task, in due course, of choosing which wall-papers we wished to have, for the house was well on towards being completed, as it was at the beginning of the road; and we began to think about an actual date for moving in. On October 24th my diary records 'last day at the office', so that I would have a free week in which to organise final details for the great day, now fixed for Wednesday, 5th November — a day of non-stop sunshine and the day on which, sleeping in our own home for the first time, I really felt that the war was over. It being Guy Fawkes' night, the sky was lit up with fireworks, and a huge bonfire on the waste ground nearby, where the Crusaders always had a grand display; and we certainly had plenty to celebrate that night! Truly, the lights had all come on once more.

And this is where I shall finish my story — except to add, by way of a postscript, that it has not been my intention to attempt to write a factual history of the war in Wallington, or at national level; but simply to recount my own experiences as a young wife

28 Hamilton Way, newly-built in 1947, the post-war home of the author and her husband.

caught up in the throes of war-time life, as recorded in my own diaries (which have been faithfully kept ever since I was a small child). I am not sure whether I really succeeded in 'smiling through' but it was not for the want of trying, and hoping all the time for the better days to come. When, after the victory, the newsreels revealed all the ghastly horrors of the Nazi concentration camps, the war did seem justified. I do recall that Sir Winston Churchill's immortal speeches seemed to inspire and cheer us on from time to time; and I carried in my mind his special phrase about 'reaching the sunlit uplands' after all the blood, sweat and tears. By some dreadful irony, there now seems to be almost a yearning for 'that kind of war' if war must come again, as compared with the ghastly finality of the nuclear holocaust now threatened. At least, then, we felt that we were struggling to maintain and preserve our culture and traditions: now we know there can be nothing to follow if the worst happens. I have found it a very emotional experience, uncovering all the events and feelings of those far-away years; but, at the end of it all, one is left with deep feelings of gratitude for all the blessings of peace and freedom which we in this country have since enjoyed as the result of the sacrifices and endurance of those who were part of the struggle for our survival.

January, 1983.

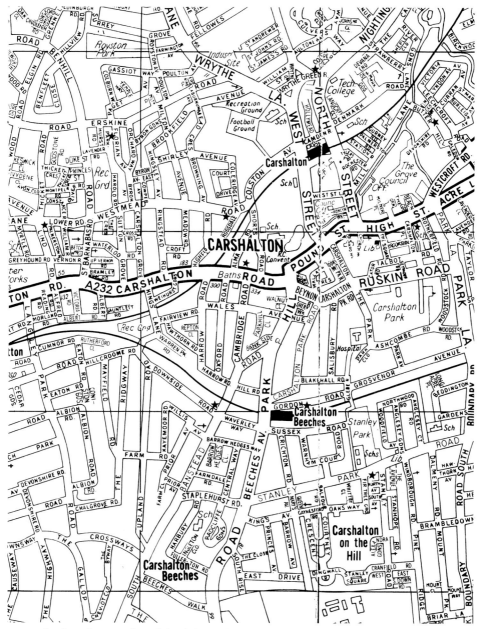

Section of street plan of Carshalton, showing some of the locations mentioned in the text. (continued overleaf).

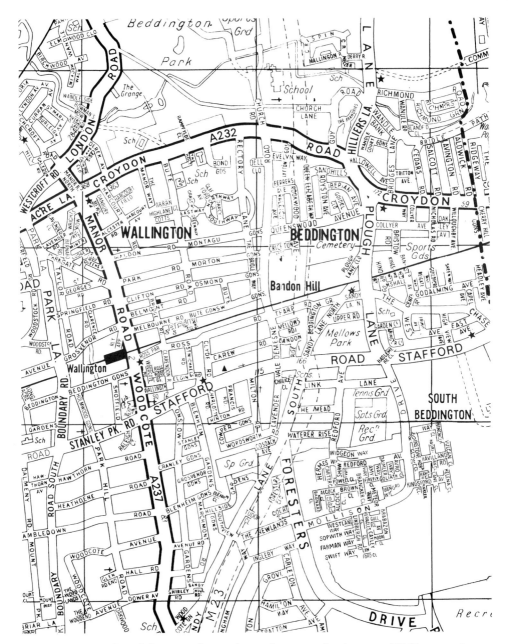

A continuation of the street plan on the previous page, showing part of Wallington and Beddington.